For Ann

[signature]

May 17, 1998

ON A WING
&
A PRAYER

On a Wing & a Prayer

Devotions for Busy Christians

• • • • • • • • • • • •

BRIAN KELLEY BAUKNIGHT

DIMENSIONS
FOR LIVING

NASHVILLE

ON A WING AND A PRAYER

Copyright © 1998 by Dimensions for Living

Library of Congress Cataloging-in-Publication Data

Bauknight, Brian Kelley, 1939–
    On a wing & a prayer: devotions for busy Christians / Brian
Kelley Bauknight.
        p.   cm.
    ISBN 0-687-05211-4 (pbk.: alk. paper)
    1. Meditations.   2. Prayers.   I. Title.
BV4832.2.B346   1998
242—dc21   97-44055
                                                                    CIP

This book is printed on acid-free paper.

98 99 00 01 02 03 04 05 06 07 — 10 9 8 7 6 5 4 3 2 1

For Jim and Marian:

mentors in the early years;

affirming and cherished friends for thirty-seven years

CONTENTS

●●●●●●●●●●●●

INTRODUCTION

●●●●●●●●●●●●

Life can be hectic. The pace of life can be frenetic. Those who choose to live as Christian disciples frequently find little time to cultivate the spiritual dimensions of the journey. Personal resolutions toward daily prayer, Scripture reading, devotional reading, worship participation, and quiet moments are broken and renewed regularly.

This book is intended to help fill the gaps. Herein are devotional helps for those who need occasional stopgap resources when time and focus become scarce. I welcome this type of book in my own pilgrimage—especially when I falter in my own covenant to a sustained spiritual discipline. I am all too familiar with crowded days and incomplete lists of "urgent" things to do. I am maturing in wisdom regarding such things. But I still need help.

My earnest hope—through this book—is for substantial spiritual encouragement in your life. For many years,

I have known that one of my spiritual gifts is encouragement. These pages contain heartening images from my life and ministry. Images and stories carry much of the best in Christian tradition. The images within these pages draw upon experiences from my life as a servant leader, a pastor, a backyard gardener, an extended family member, and one Christian traveler. Each numbered piece contains a "wing"—a word to lift, guide, challenge, or direct your daily walk. A prayer focus or brief prayer follows—a guide to move you from reading to the business of living. Interspersed throughout are uplifting texts from Scripture. Occasionally I include texts from other writings—sayings that have nurtured and encouraged me.

Discipleship is the overall theme. As Christians, discipleship is our mission. The images presented here focus on three primary discipleship issues: worship, devotional life, and stewardship—those which John Wesley called "acts of piety." For the most part, I have not included here the other critical piece of discipleship—what Wesley called "works of mercy." Disciples also are called to exercise mercy—acts of compassion and justice. Although essential to a holistic Christian life, these issues of outreach are left for another time—or another book.

The size of this book is deliberate: small, for your desktop, briefcase, carry-on luggage, or laptop computer case. Here is a book that is easy to carry with you wherever you may go.

As you begin to read or browse through this book, I pray that these brief devotions will provide spiritual nurture and upbuilding for your life.

—Brian Kelley Bauknight

ON A WING
& A PRAYER

1. SOARING

•••••••••••••

A great teacher once noted the distinctions among flying, gliding, and soaring. The images are indelibly imprinted upon my memory. In flying, you are powered through the air, by powerful engines that produce thrust. In gliding, you are towed to your launch height; then you float back to the earth. In soaring, however, you pay attention to the thermal currents that lift you and carry you along. You pay attention to the wind. Isaiah must have had something like this in mind when he wrote, "Those who wait for the LORD . . . shall mount up with wings like eagles" (Isaiah 40:31).

The Christian life is much like soaring. When you pay close attention to the winds of the Spirit of God, you are carried to new heights and over great distances not otherwise possible.

Watch and wait for the refreshing, restorative power God offers. To catch that wind and let God lift you is no longer only an issue of possibility. It is an issue of necessity and survival. To soar is to know exhilaration in the life of faith.

Prayer Focus: Close your eyes and imagine the experience of soaring, upheld by God's Spirit.

Those who wait for the LORD *shall renew their strength, / they shall mount up with wings like eagles, / they shall run and not be weary, / they shall walk and not faint.*

(Isaiah 40:31)

2. FAX FROM THE FUTURE

• • • • • • • • • • • •

Fax machines are now a necessity in any modern office. A colleague recently recounted an interesting experience with a fax. Members of his church who were living in Australia sent him a fax. He read it, and then he noticed the date of the fax transmission. It was dated—and sent—*tomorrow.* The fax was sent *the day after* he received it—because of Australia's time zone. He dubbed the letter his "fax from the future."

God is calling to you *from* the future and *into* the future with increasing persuasiveness. God is sending you "future messages" about what it means to be a child of God, to be a disciple of Jesus.

None of us can manage, control, or manipulate the future. However, God calls you and then guides you toward the call. God is always ahead of you, inviting you toward a richer, nobler life in Christ.

Prayer Focus: "Image" where God may be calling you and your life right now. Ask God to refine and perfect that image.

> *He is the image of the invisible God. . . . He himself is before all things, and in him all things hold together.*
>
> (Colossians 1:15, 17)

3. TIME WARP

•••••••••••

We were vacationing late in the summer in Williamsburg, Virginia. While I was browsing in a video store one evening, a woman walked into the store who seemed totally out of context. She was in full colonial costume—head to toe, bonnet to high-buckle shoe. She was a woman of the eighteenth century perusing the technology and entertainment of the twentieth century.

I sensed some kind of time warp. The woman seemed oblivious to the incongruity of the moment. She pulled two movies from the shelf, paid with a credit card, exchanged a warm smile and greeting with the clerk, and bustled out of the store. I was tempted to follow her to see whether she left in an ox-drawn cart or a convertible!

Christian faith transcends time and technology. Our challenge is to connect our faith journey with modern realities. Sometimes such connecting seems almost as incongruous as a Colonial Williamsburg woman browsing a display of movie videos. Yet the gospel has the power to make that connection—and more.

Connecting with Jesus is a timeless gift, cutting across matters of culture or historical moment. Everything holds together in Christ. The timelessness of God's Word and way in the world is cause for celebration and hope!

Prayer Focus: Ask God to connect some disjointed part of your life with Eternal purpose.

4. A NEW LANGUAGE

●●●●●●●●●●●●●

Our four-year-old granddaughter played with the other preschoolers in the children's pool near Disney World. She engaged in animated conversation with another child for a few minutes. She looked puzzled, even a bit confused, but she maintained a steady flow of words. The other child responded with equal energy.

After a short while, our granddaughter left the pool and ran over to her mother. She looked worried about something. "Mommy," she said, pointing to her new friend, "that little girl can't talk."

"Of course she can talk," came the reply. "I saw the two of you talking just now." Reality suddenly dawned. The other child was speaking French. She was one of many non-English-speaking visitors to Disney World.

Our little granddaughter reflected for a few seconds, then plunged back into the pool to resume play. No lack of communication would deter her from a new friendship.

Many persons whom you know do not easily assimilate words such as *prayer, grace, spiritual,* or even *church.* Our world does not naturally speak the language of faith.

Countless persons are ensnared in encroaching secularization. They have little knowledge of religious tradition. Their children have never been to church. They have never knelt at the Lord's Table. The Bible is a mystery, and no clues exist to unravel the mystery.

If we are to effectively reach out in Christ's name, we must do so with a new language. The language will not always *sound* religious, yet it will be deeply communicative of the love of God. It will be the language of touch, of symbols, and of a contagious smile. It will be a language that opens doors through which Jesus Christ can walk.

Prayer Focus: Ask God for adequate words to speak to the real needs of one person you meet today.

It is not for us to prophesy the day, but the day will come when [Christians] will be called to utter the truth of God with such power as will change and renew the world.

(Dietrich Bonhoeffer,
Prisoner for God)

5. BOTHERED BY THE SPIRIT

●●●●●●●●●●●●

Recently, our church's worship bulletin had a memorable misprint. An affirmation of faith read: "Jesus Christ . . . works in us and *bothers* by the Spirit." Obviously, the letter "b" was an inadvertent addition. Neither our computer's spell-check program nor careful proofreading had caught the error.

The rich truth is clear, however: We *ought* to be bothered by the Spirit! At least somewhat. In a world gone mad with secular pursuits, the Spirit needs to bother us—into a new awareness, a new perspective, a new boldness.

Someone has suggested that when people show in their public lives that their faith matters to them, they risk ridicule as well as actual punishment. This culture does not understand the work of the holy, the divine mystery, the Spirit in the midst of life.

It has been said that a "yawning hole" persists in our nation's psyche, that a vacuum inhabits the heart of the American character. To know the wealth of Christian hope and spiritual satisfaction is precisely what fills this empty void.

Will you allow yourself to be *bothered* by the Spirit of

God? Will you allow that same Spirit to quietly but persuasively dominate how you think and act in both public and private life?

Prayer Focus: Lean into God for a few moments. Yearn for a connection with the Spirit of God in such a way as to know the constancy of God's presence.

> *God is spirit, and those who worship him must worship in spirit and truth.*
>
> (John 4:24)

6. NEEDLED BY THE EYE OF A CAMEL

●●●●●●●●●●●●

A poster contains a photograph of the face of a camel. His chin rests on a wall in the foreground. His face is incredibly ugly, with huge jowls, a sagging mouth, and loose skin hanging everywhere. His eyes have a deep, questioning look. The caption beneath the picture reads, "Does anyone really know what time it is?"

Do the eyes of that camel speak a question you secretly ask? We are always conscious of the time. But do you really know what time it is?

In the Bible, time is not measured by duration, but by meaning. This seemingly subtle difference is quite extraordinary. Biblical people were not ruled by passing moments and hours. Rather, they sought to find meaning and purpose in the time allotted to them.

So much of what we are about seems to block this reality from our lives. The hustle and din, the wheeling and dealing of our lives distorts our understanding of time.

Is this the reason for the sadness in the eyes of my poster camel? Have we missed the profound wisdom in his eyes?

Jesus reminds you and me that "the time is fulfilled"

(Mark 1:15). He calls us into a new awareness of time. Paul writes similarly, "Be careful then how you live, not as unwise people but as wise, making the most of the time" (Ephesians 5:15).

It is time for you and me to live as though Jesus Christ has come. It is time to live as though his coming makes a difference. Know what time it is—in *your* life!

Prayer Focus: God, nudge me toward knowing "what time it is" and what is most important for me to accomplish today.

7. WHATEVER THIS DAY MAY BRING

● ● ● ● ● ● ● ● ● ● ● ● ●

Dietrich Bonhoeffer sustained fellow prisoners in Germany during the last three years of his life. His faith and witness were remarkable and memorable. I am told that a few months before his execution in 1945, Bonhoeffer wrote this message in his journal: "Lord, whatever this day may bring, thy Name be praised."

What a beautiful way to begin every new day. Try it!

Prayer Focus: Meditate upon Bonhoeffer's prayer. Then pray it aloud several times. Jot it on a note and place the note in a prominent place today.

> *The LORD is good to all, / and his compassion is over all that he has made.*
>
> (Psalm 145:9)

8. THE CARDINAL

•••••••••••••

A bird feeder hangs just outside my office window from early fall until late spring. During the "snow and ice" days of early spring, the feeder is a busy gathering place for many sparrows and an occasional chickadee.

On one of the coldest snow-covered mornings, there was an unusually high activity level in the area of the feeder. More than a dozen sparrows were playing, trying to keep warm, searching the snow for fallen food, jostling for position on the feeding tray. It was a microcosm of the world—human beings playing, jostling for position, vying for limited space and supplies of food.

Then I noticed him: a glorious cardinal perched high above the limb on which the feeder hung. He watched with a kind of majestic silence. The brightness of his red coat brought a startling contrast to the white of the frozen garden landscape. He made no attempt to interfere or make a place for himself. He merely sat in quiet splendor and observed.

Whether or not the sparrows felt his presence, I do not know. Those of us watching through the window surely did.

Above the noise, the competition, the strife, and the busyness of this life reigns the Risen Christ. He has lived among us. He knows the frustrations and the limitations you face. He knows the temptation to push others away, the propensity for greed, and the inevitability of some exploitation. Yet he has conquered all of life and all of death. And now he watches over you in love.

The Risen Christ reigns over life with invincible splendor.

Prayer Focus: Close your eyes and "see" the risen Christ watching over you right now. Ask his special guidance or instruction for the remainder of the day.

> *You who live in the shelter of the Most High, / who abide in the shadow of the Almighty, / will say to the LORD, "My refuge and my fortress; / my God, in whom I trust."*
>
> (Psalm 91:1-2)

9. OUT OF CONTROL

•••••••••••••

The call came from my cardiologist early one Friday afternoon. He had just read the tapes of the twenty-four-hour heart monitor I had worn the preceding day. His words came with startling bluntness: "I want you at the hospital emergency room right away, within the hour."

I attempted a feeble protest. "I have a wedding tomorrow. Can't admission wait until then? I feel fine. I will come immediately after the wedding."

"I wish I could agree," he replied, "but it simply would not be fair to tell you that this can wait. There are too many dangerous possibilities here."

So began an unsettling sequence of events in which I increasingly turned over control of my "earthly vessel" to a host of specialized "others." Medical delivery and testing came at a furious pace: the emergency room staff; a parade of physicians, interns, and residents; blood sample and I.V. technicians; and highly trained CCU and IMCU nurses. With amazing speed, my control of time and mobility, my food choices and contacts with the outside world were lost. Life seemed to suddenly go out of control.

"Not so!" thunders the psalmist of faith. In the providence of God, life is never out of control. Nothing in all creation diminishes the care and complete control of

36

God. "O God, you are my God / . . . . My soul is satisfied as with a rich feast, / . . . when I think of you / . . . . Your right hand upholds me" (Psalm 63:1-8).

The window of faith allows you to see any situation with new eyes. The God who is unequivocally with you all the days of your life is a very present help and very much in charge, even in the strange world of the hospital. Through the doubts, through the probing and pinching, through the poking and prying, through the decisions that one must make, the God of our Lord Jesus Christ is in control.

Prayer Focus: Ask for the ability to give yourself absolutely to God's sustaining care at all times.

10. POKING HOLES IN THE DARKNESS

• • • • • • • • • • • •

A story by Robert Louis Stevenson records a moment from his childhood. He gazed through a window upon a dark winter evening as the lamp-lighter came down the street lighting the gas lamps. He called out to his mother, "Mother, look. I see something wonderful. There's a man coming down the street poking holes in the dark."

That is precisely why Jesus came. Jesus continues to desire a breakthrough in your life: to poke holes in the dark, so that you can get in touch with the light, so that you can connect and reconnect with God.

This is the promise and the plan of God. Reliability is assured.

Prayer Focus: "Image" the divine "Lamp-Lighter" in your mind's eye—poking holes in any segments of your darkness.

The light shines in the darkness, and the darkness did not overcome it.

(John 1:5)

---

11. CREEPING KUDZU

•••••••••••••

Kudzu is taking over. The plant variety, that is, not the cartoon strip featuring the preacher with the wide-brimmed hat! In the southeastern United States, kudzu is everywhere. The large, rapidly growing vines sometimes cover the trees for miles along the interstates and the blue highways of North and South Carolina, Georgia, and other states. In its advanced state, the nearly "finished product" resembles a rather attractive sculpture over the landscape of woodlands.

But the attractive appearance is deceptive. Kudzu spreads faster than almost any other wild plant, growing about twelve inches every twenty-four hours. Gradually, it covers a tree (or group of trees) completely. Eventually, it suffocates the tree, and the tree (or entire forest) dies.

Kudzu was imported to the United States in order to combat soil erosion. No one could foresee the unstoppable results. My uncle was a professor of agricultural economics at a southern university. Each time I visited, he would offer a few choice words for the individual who first imported kudzu to this country.

In many ways, the culture of the present moment looks rather attractive. The world of supermarkets, super malls, super sports stars, and high-tech living glitters and glistens. Unfortunately, this culture also has a tendency to take over. We are easily seduced. Soon, consumer goods and services occupy or preoccupy our time, energy, and interest.

One day, almost without warning or recognition, the precious spiritual qualities of life are smothered. The vitality of a life of faith is sapped. Human life wilts and seems to suffocate by the possession of many artifacts and toys.

Jesus came to exemplify and give an entirely new alternative. Jesus brings energy and resiliency, never sapping our spirits. His image is the opposite of the creeping kudzu.

Prayer Focus: What secular interest is sapping your energy? Invite the new energy of Christ to replace it!

12. WHEN DEPRIVED OF THE LIGHT

●●●●●●●●●●●●

A beautifully shaped blue spruce stood in stately grandeur through the changing seasons at the southwest corner of our yard. We tried to save the tree. The tree doctor informed us, however, that the tree had a disease of some kind. The disease was progressing slowly, moving up from ground level. There was no known cure.

Reluctantly, I gave in. With the assistance of a friend, the majestic spruce was felled one early summer day.

We immediately became aware of an additional problem. The gap left by the felled tree exposed the interior sides of the bordering evergreens. Those evergreen branches were now brown and dead. The spruce tree had blocked the light.

"Never mind," I thought out loud. "In a season or two, the green will reappear, the evergreens will fill out once again, and the barren places will no longer be an eyesore."

"Not so," reflected my friend. He seemed to know. "Once deprived of the light for a long period of time, the shrub will live, but it will no longer grow on that side."

His wisdom was prophetic. After several seasons, the light-deprived evergreens remained brown and lifeless on the side where the great tree once stood.

If we deprive ourselves of the light for a few years, do we cease to grow? Without light, there is no growth, no greening, and no new shoots of fresh promise.

Medical researchers are now beginning to posit what some physicians have observed for years. Certain people become depressed and withdrawn when sunlight is unavailable to them for extended periods of time. Such persons survive, but the vibrancy of life is periodically lost.

Jesus as Light is the critical ingredient for healthy living. We need full exposure to that light all our days.

Prayer Focus: May I always remain open to the One who is the Light of Life.

God is light and in him there is no darkness at all.
(1 John 1:5)

---

13. TWO LEFT FEET

•••••••••••

I arrived in Washington, D.C., for a major national convocation. I was providing partial leadership through a long weekend of lectures, small group meetings, and worship. I had eagerly anticipated the event for many months.

I received my room assignment, moved my luggage to the room, and began to unpack. Reaching into my shoe bag, I pulled out two black dress shoes. Something seemed amiss. Suddenly I realized what I had done. *I had packed two left shoes!* Same color. Same style. But both for the left foot. The alternative was a pair of informal canvas walking shoes!

Humbled and embarrassed, I made the best of it. I gave my presentation, preached a morning service, and led reflection groups in canvas walking shoes. Fortunately, informal attire was the order of the day.

I felt pretty foolish. Yet I was accepted and received throughout—not even a hint of criticism or ridicule. The event proceeded smoothly.

How great to know a God who loves me, even when I appear with two left feet! How refreshing to know that I do not have to appear before my Maker in perfected dress and impeccable good order! I am received, affirmed, and welcomed because I am God's creation. I hold membership in a noble spiritual family. The klutzy clumsiness of my endeavors are never maligned. God asks me to strive for greater obedience *precisely because* I am greatly loved.

I will undoubtedly forget something else another travel time: a belt, a matching tie, even a suit. But I will always know that God is not embarrassed or put off by my human limitations. In fact, God probably loves me best when I stand utterly shoeless in the Holy Presence!

Prayer: Thank you, Lord, for your gracious acceptance of me for who I am right now!

One thing I asked of the LORD, / that will I seek after: / to live in the house of the LORD / all the days of my life, / to behold the beauty of the LORD, / and to inquire in his temple.

(Psalm 27:4)

14. THE SINGING DOES NOT STOP!

● ● ● ● ● ● ● ● ● ● ● ●

Some years ago, a venerable tradition ended in our home. For fifteen years, our four children were in some level of public school education. Each weekday morning during the school year, they were awakened for breakfast with a song newly created by their father! It was a noble tradition that I received from my own father and desired to pass down to the next generation!

The morning wake-up song stopped on the day our youngest son completed high school. All four children had wished the singing would stop much sooner. They were never lavish in their praise of the tradition or of my voice. In fact, quite the opposite was true!

To be sure, my morning vocalizing was not of the highest quality. (Some say I sing like a prisoner: behind a few bars and without a key!) Usually I created some unpolished impromptu poetry in the shower, adapting the words to a familiar hymn tune or seasonal carol. Once dressed and "rehearsed," I sang it boldly.

My music received the expected groans of protest for fifteen years. In fact, at least two of our children tried all kinds of persuasive techniques to make the singing stop much earlier. (My sisters and I tried similar persuasions with my father a generation earlier!)

The Christian faith is a morning faith—not literally, of course; but in rich symbolism. A favorite poster hangs behind my office desk: "He has turned our sunsets into sunrise." A favorite quotation from Dietrich Bonhoeffer reads, "The dawn belongs to the Church of the Risen Christ."

You are promised some bright new dawnings on your faith journey. Those dawnings can cause you to break forth into song. Sometimes the song is better sung in the shower or on the road, but it is song nonetheless.

May this day be filled with music and—even if you are not a morning person—may you join in the singing.

Prayer Focus: When alone for a few moments today, try singing aloud a hymn or Christian song of memory. If you don't know one, make one up!

He put a new song in my mouth, / a song of praise to our God. / Many will see and fear, / and put their trust in the LORD.

(Psalm 40:3)

15. DISLOCATION

••••••••••••

A newspaper article told of a man who was driving west from New Mexico *and totally missed the state of Arizona!* He ended up on the shore of the Pacific Ocean at the end of an interstate highway. A California highway patrolman found the man sitting in the car with a puzzled look on his face and a map open on the seat beside him. When asked how he missed the entire state of Arizona, the man replied that he did not know, but he had been under a lot of stress lately!

Have you ever felt you might be at the center of a story like that? A lot of us spend most of our waking hours somewhere between "busyness" and "weariness." We race through long hours of long days. We find little time for refreshment or replenishment.

Sociologists remind us of something we already know: The number of hours we work has increased about 20 percent since 1974. In contrast, the hours we spend in leisure have decreased by more than 30 percent. A huge number of complex choices clog our already crowded schedules. Sometimes we think we are coming unglued.

Claim God's promise for you. In Christ, all things hold together.

Prayer Focus: Allow God to hold your weariness. Ask God to hold it permanently.

> *I will sing of your might; / I will sing aloud of your steadfast love in the morning.*
>
> (Psalm 59:16)

16. FAMILY REUNION

•••••••••••••

A boy went reluctantly to the annual family reunion. He didn't want to go, mostly because of the small number of children his age who would be there. On this particular occasion, he wandered among the small clusters of family members and listened intently to the subjects under discussion. Later, when he went to bed that night, he said this prayer: "Dear God, bless Mommy and Daddy, and bless all of these people who are coming apart at the seams."

Sometimes, those words seem the best description of a week, a month, or a year. Perhaps that description fits you right now.

Then listen! God promises to Jeremiah: "I will satisfy the weary, / and all who are faint I will replenish" (31:25). What an offer! Accept the offer as God's gift to you right now!

Prayer Focus: Close your eyes and let the words from Jeremiah roll over you like a cool stream of water on a very hot day.

17. POWER-AID

••••••••••••

The pattern is predictable. A football player runs off the field after a particularly difficult series of downs—or after a big play. What happens next? He reaches for a long drink of Gatorade. A supply stands ready on every football field at every game—at least the televised ones!

My two grandsons play Little League baseball. They have a new sports drink to model that of the professionals. It's called Powerade.

Marketing strategists know exactly what they are doing. The overt message speaks clearly: You will receive power surging through you; you will receive refreshment when you drink this beverage.

Some people seem to have boundless energy—to love, trust, encourage, work, study, and believe—while others seem to quickly run out of steam. Why do some people have all the power they need while others have hardly any?

Perhaps it is necessary to look more deeply within to find a source for their power. Is there an energy that unifies? Is there some inner strength?

Scripture gives a strong, positive answer to that question. We do not reach down for some extra boost. Rather, we reach down—or out, or up—to take the hand of God.

In taking that hand, we are refreshed for the journey. God offers what a quick fix of Gatorade or Powerade can never deliver. God offers a source of energy that never runs dry *because it is divine energy.*

Evelyn Underhill is said to have told her students, "We must find the source of strength and renewal for our spirits lest we perish." Those words were never more true than right now. Find that source for you today and rejoice.

Prayer Focus: Form the preceding quotation into a prayer for your life: "God, help me to find the source of strength and renewal for my life, beginning today!" Make a short list of what God's Spirit suggests are the best "sources" for you.

But you will receive power when the Holy Spirit has come upon you.

(Acts 1:8*a*)

---

18. FULLNESS OF JOY

●●●●●●●●●●●●

A friend of mine is a wonderful storyteller. He has an extraordinary sense of humor—always in good taste. His confidence in God and the centrality of Jesus Christ in his life are consistent and evident.

A few years ago he was struck with a crippling, degenerative illness. No cure is forthcoming. Decreasing bodily function is inevitable.

Shortly after his diagnosis, he addressed a major denominational group. Many had asked him "how he was doing" in light of his illness.

He spoke with a firm and confident voice: "You ask how I am doing? I can tell you this: *I am determined that nothing will ever take away my joy!*"

Marvelous! That is exactly the way things are meant to be in God's kingdom. Paul reminds us that the sufferings of this present time are not worth comparing to the joy that is to be revealed to us!

What a great truth by which to live. Evil, suffering, and injustice are never the last word. Resiliency empowers the believer. Nothing in all of creation will ever take away your joy.

God's promise rings through the words of Isaiah: "For you shall go out in joy" (55:12).

Prayer: Grant, O God, that nothing that happens to me or around me shall ever diminish or erase the joy of knowing you.

> *In all these things we are more than conquerors through him who loved us.*
>
> (Romans 8:37)

19. ONE OF THOSE DAYS

••••••••••••

A kindergarten teacher dreaded days of rain and snow. Such days always meant thirty pairs of overshoes to put on and take off several times. At the end of one particularly snowy day, she struggled repeatedly with each child's pair of overshoes. The last child was an especially difficult fit. She worked and worked. Finally, she got the boots on his feet. At that moment, the little boy said, "Those aren't my boots."

Summoning all the patience she could muster, the teacher dutifully removed the boots with considerable effort. When they were off, the boy looked at her and said, "They are my sister's. But my mom said I had to wear them today anyway."

Have you ever had days like that? Found yourself in such situations? Only by leaning into God's energy do we discover a power that exceeds all expectations. Paul knew of that power when he wrote, "I can do all things through [him] who strengthens me" (Philippians 4:13).

Prayer: Merciful God, bring me special strength for difficult and unexpected situations. Let your exceeding strength be my source of hope and encouragement for this day.

> *My foot stands on level ground; / in the great congregation I will bless the LORD.*
>
> (Psalm 26:12)

20. MASTER
OF YOUR SOUL?

• • • • • • • • • • • •

He was forty years older than me. He died at the age of ninety-five. His influence on my spiritual pilgrimage cannot be adequately measured.

He was the first preacher I ever knew. I was four years old when he came to my home church. I do not recall much of the content of his messages—except for one powerful line. I can still hear the resonant sound of his voice today: "I do not care how many skills you master in this life, but I do care who is the Master of your soul."

Memorable words, worthy of reflection and appreciation. Jesus wants to be the Master of your soul—today, tomorrow, and all the days ahead.

Prayer Focus: Offer yourself to be mastered by the Master of Galilee. In a moment of silence, extend your hand into his hand—one that is already outstretched toward you.

> *Therefore, since we are receiving a kingdom that cannot be shaken, let us give thanks, by which we offer to God an acceptable worship with reverence and awe.* (Hebrews 12:28)

21. TICKETS, PLEASE!

●●●●●●●●●●●●●

A friend tells of finding a "quarterly ticket" in his great-great-grandmother's Bible. The ticket is dated A.D. 1884, and signed by her Methodist preacher. Once each quarter, the circuit-riding preacher came through the small towns to boost the faithful and verify patterns of attendance. Two signatures verified that the member had been faithful in worship attendance at his or her church during the most recent three-month period.

Can you imagine collecting tickets for a worship service today? We can scarcely contemplate the power or the discipline of such behavior.

Such faithfulness is difficult to sustain in our day. Weekend leisure becomes the norm. "Night and day" sales draw huge crowds to the shopping malls. Leisure theme parks lure us and then remake us into tired, grumpy people. Skilled manipulators find fresh ways to entice consumption of our discretionary time.

In order to be "card carrying" believers today, you need great intentionality. I believe it was James Smart who said, "Worship is the Christian's vital breath." Be sure you breathe well this week!

Prayer: God, grant me the vital breath of worship with a community of believers in the coming days.

> *So shall my word be that goes out from my mouth; / it shall not return to me empty, / but it shall accomplish that which I purpose, / and succeed in the thing for which I sent it.*
>
> (Isaiah 55:11)

22. GONE FISHING

●●●●●●●●●●●●

The disciples of Jesus gathered after Easter Day. The One who gave them "reason for being" had been taken from their midst. They were at odds with themselves as to what to do next. I imagine a conversation along these lines:

What are you going to do now?
I don't know. What are *you* going to do?

I hear this conversation repeated again, several times! Can you hear them?

Finally, Peter interrupts the inane discussion. "Well, I know what I am going to do. I am going fishing! The Galilee Fishing Commission started selling permits yesterday. I got mine. And I am going fishing."

The three-year adventure was over. Jesus was gone from their midst. The disciples undoubtedly were subject to some ridicule. "Ho! The great adventurers are back in your boats, are you?"

Those who had been with Jesus were emotionally drained. They tried to stay "high," but they were unable to maintain enthusiasm—until Jesus came among them one more time.

In a *Peanuts* cartoon, Lucy and Charlie Brown are

talking. Charlie Brown says, "I don't know, Lucy, I'm really feeling down today."

"Well, Charlie Brown," she says, "you know that life has its ups and downs."

"But I don't want any downs," he replies. "I just want ups and ups and ups."

Life is neither easy nor predictable. But God is steadfast. In your most unsteady times, Jesus stands alongside you. He invites you into a relationship that endures into eternity. That invitation and your response reflect the very essence of life.

Prayer: God, grant me a resilient spirit in all situations—especially those I may face today.

23. PRAYER CHANGES THINGS

•••••••••••

A woman purchased an antique plaque that fit nicely into the decor of her home. It read simply, "Prayer changes things!" She brought the plaque home and hung it above the mantel over the fireplace. The next day, she noticed that the plaque was missing. When she inquired of her husband about the matter, he told her that he had taken it down. "What's the matter?" she asked. "Don't you believe in prayer?"

"Sure I believe in prayer," he replied. "I just don't like change."

Change disrupted the life of my wife and me on a cold winter night in January 1994. A violent auto collision occurred, shattering her hip and foot. The other driver was D.U.I.

The next twelve to eighteen months were more difficult than any we had ever known. My wife suffered excruciating pain. My own disciplined, ordered way of doing things was significantly altered.

I do not thrive well on disruptive change. A daily and weekly routine guides my writing, my preparations for preaching, my support and encouragement of staff, and my pastoral work.

Without question, prayer was the undergirding power for both of us in the face of change. Prayer sustained us: prayer for bodily healing, for injured bones and tissues, for restoration of blood flow; prayer for patience while the healing power flowed; prayer for inner healing of the memories of that night.

Prayer changes things. Prayer releases a flow of divine energy. Prayer changes lives. Prayer changed our lives.

Prayer will not necessarily undo physical and emotional injury. But prayer will sustain you for the days ahead.

Prayer Focus: Ask God for renewed confidence in the use of prayer in your life.

Rejoice in hope, be patient in suffering, persevere in prayer.

(Romans 12:12)

---

24. A TURN AT BAT

••••••••••••

On a leisurely drive home from work, a man stopped to watch a few minutes of a Little League baseball game. Caught up in the excitement of the game, he got out of the car and stood behind one of the dugouts. Finally, he asked a boy from the team in the dugout, "What's the score?"

"Fourteen to zero," the boy replied—with a huge smile and enthusiasm in his voice. "The other team is ahead!"

"You're behind 14-0?" the man asked. "Then why are you so happy?"

The reply was classic: "Mister, our team hasn't come up to bat yet!"

No matter how far down life takes us, we are never in despair. In Christ, hope will never disappoint us. A victory that matters is ultimately assured.

Prayer: God, give me the confident victory in Christ. Grant me the maturity of a childlike faith.

Endurance produces character, and character produces hope, and hope does not disappoint us.
                                    (Romans 5:4-5a)

---

25. SUPERNOVA

●●●●●●●●●●●●

An exciting discovery was announced by a small group of astronomers. Students of the night sky observed a new, explosive blaze of light hundreds of thousands of light years into space. With powerful telescopes trained on the light, they presumed it to be the infrequently seen explosion of a dying star.

Enthusiasm in the scientific community grew rapidly. A rare opportunity now existed to learn something about the formation of the universe. Researchers could test some long-standing theories about the origins of celestial space. Mysteries heretofore relegated to speculation would be unclouded. Humankind would have answers that had been elusive.

For several days, the newspaper reports and interviews spoke of what astronomers would learn. Suddenly, the news stories stopped. Press releases ceased. What happened? This supernova did not conform to known data. Confusion and enigma returned. Scientists would need to reexamine data and adjust their theories. The chance of any definitive explanation was slim. All bets regarding certainty were off!

The news of Jesus' resurrection refuses to be categorized or classified according to existing guidelines. Mystery endures, even for the believer.

Jesus encounters you in personal, unexplainable, unreserved mystery. Yet he does come! You can only reexamine your life in the blazing light of his risen glory.

Prayer: Thank you, Lord Jesus, for the mystery and power of the Easter event. Let the Risen Christ be a part of this day in my life.

26. FRUITCAKE

•••••••••••••

Every holiday season, someone declares open season on fruitcake. Critics take to the print media, cartoon pages, radio talk shows, and other settings in hopes of fruitcake annihilation.

One recent Thanksgiving season, the harangue renewed with fresh enthusiasm. Someone advertised a fruitcake hurling contest—like a shot-put! Another wrote of the unexpected arrival at his home of the perfect material for repair of a brick wall. (An alternative would be to use it as a tire chock or door stop.) A morning radio host gave instructions on fruitcake waste management. Another blithely announced that anyone giving or receiving a fruitcake in the next two months must file an environmental impact statement with the EPA!

The word went out from a recent space flight mission that fruitcake failed the anti-gravity test in space: it sank to the bottom of the cabin *when there was no gravity!*

I happen to like fruitcake! Not all brands, mind you. Not the kind that turns to sugar (or worse) in a few weeks. But I do like at least one brand, made with natural fruit, flour, spices, and no sugar added. Actually healthier than a lot of the sweets we consume, this fruitcake contains nuts, raisins, dried fruit, and whole wheat flour.

Sometimes ugly or unexpected events land in the midst of life with a highly disagreeable thud. Your first impulse is toward scorn and cynicism. You may question God's purpose or integrity for at least a moment.

But, upon examination, you discover this same event to be filled with God's goodness. From a Christian's eye-view, there is always a strong possibility that more good is present in the substance of life than meets the eye. When you try to see events through God's eye-view, the possibility for good is exceedingly high.

Prayer Focus: Invite God to show you the good in a recent difficult, confusing, or negative situation. Invite God to work toward that good through you.

I sought the LORD *and he answered me, / and delivered me from all my fears."*

(Psalm 34:4)

27. A STORM AT SEA

• • • • • • • • • • • •

Sometimes I understand why Jesus needed to calm the storm for a group of frightened disciples. Even in the life of faith, storms have a way of unraveling us for a while.

Blaise Pascal, French mathematician and philosopher, is said to have written these memorable words: "It is a great thing to be on a ship in a storm-tossed sea when one knows that the ship will not sink."

When I feel tempest-tossed and battered, I often think of these words.

Prayer Focus: Give thanks to God for absolute certainty that we are upheld in love.

For I am convinced that neither death / nor life . . . nor things present, nor things to come . . . nor height, nor depth, nor anything else in all creation, will be able to separate us from the love of God in Christ Jesus our Lord.

(Romans 8:38)

---

28. SING THE SONG

•••••••••••

The sturdy limestone walls of one church surround a beautiful and carefully planned meditation garden. The garden was the dream and the gift of one of the early saints of that congregation nearly two generations ago.

At an early hour one morning, I stood alone at the door of that garden for a while, enjoying the quiet of that moment. Suddenly the silence was broken by the uninhibited chirping of a lone robin. Her music echoed off the stone and glass surroundings in an especially beautiful melody.

Easter happened first in a garden. On a quiet morning, centuries ago, a lone triumphal song broke forth. And the music has been echoing from the hills and valleys of life ever since.

Scholars believe that several fragments of New Testament scripture are actually from the Easter hymnody of the earliest church. (See the example following today's prayer focus.) A fragment of scripture helps us to know the song that was sung with conviction from the beginning. The church of Jesus Christ was born out of the Resurrection gospel. Hear the music of Easter each new day in your life. Hear the music in the depths of your own spirit. When you hear the music, join the singing!

Prayer Focus: Quietly repeat the following verse as a prayer for this day. Pray the prayer at least three times.

"Sleeper, awake! Rise from the dead, and Christ will shine on you."

(Ephesians 5:14)

29. COMPETING ROOT SYSTEMS

●●●●●●●●●●●●

Carefully and tediously, I began cultivating around the asparagus plants in my garden. Dead foliage was cut back to make room for new growth. Soil was loosened. Fertilizer was applied.

Suddenly I came upon a healthy green dandelion growing in the middle of a clump of asparagus roots. A few small, delicate asparagus tips were emerging and encircling the healthy dandelion. My dilemma was apparent.

Would I be able to remove the dandelion without damaging or destroying the tender young asparagus? The two could not continue to grow simultaneously. The aggressive growth of the *less* desirable would eventually crowd the *more* desirable. Could the long tap root of the weed be removed without damaging the roots of the vegetable? The root systems formed a mutually exclusive situation.

Competing systems would dominate our lives. How do we encourage an effective, sensitive, deeply caring lifestyle in the midst of affluent, sensuous, and relatively care-less secularism? How do we support and nurture responsible personhood in the midst of growing selfishness and self-centered isolation?

My specific gardening problem on that Spring day required a long, slender root knife to remove the destructive weed. I could only hope that whatever injury was caused by removing the unwanted plant would heal.

Decidedly, the rooting of life requires great care, attention, and sensitivity. God grant you a productive life, firmly rooted in his love.

Prayer: Lord God, clarify the competing root systems of my life. Help me nurture those which produce growth toward you.

I pray that, according to the riches of his glory, he may grant that you may be strengthened in your inner being with power through his Spirit, and that Christ may dwell in your hearts through faith, as you are being rooted and grounded in love.
(Ephesians 3:16-17)

30. REAL FOOD

● ● ● ● ● ● ● ● ● ● ● ●

We were visiting retired friends on Hilton Head Island. They had been informal "grandparents" to our children before moving to this new location.

He was an avid fisherman. She was an outstanding cook. In particular, she knew ways to prepare seafood as a culinary delight.

He took me and our two young sons fishing and crabbing. That night, we had a seafood feast unparalleled in my experience. Fresh from the sea in varied forms and cooking styles! The meal was memorable.

The next day, we headed north for home. About noon, we stopped at a fast-food restaurant for lunch. Our youngest son offered editorial comment from the back seat: "Oh, finally, some *real* food." The exceptional eating experience of the previous evening had totally escaped him.

Don't ever let "fast" or "quick" be a substitute for the deeper tastes of life. The psalmist invites you to "taste and see that the LORD is good" (Psalm 34:8). Such tasting takes time and preparation. But it is worth every minute spent in preparation and in savoring.

Perhaps you can have lunch today or tomorrow in a place where you can savor the food a bit—a reminder of the manner in which you can come to know God.

Prayer: God, let me take the time to know you. Let my experience with you today be more than a fast-food intake.

31. DEEP AND WIDE

●●●●●●●●●●●●

An old gospel song and Sunday school chorus uses a repeated refrain: "Deep and wide, deep and wide. . . ." The song is particularly popular with little children because they can gesture "deep" and "wide" with their tiny hands and arms.

The phrase "deep and wide" is an apt description of the direction for every Christian pilgrim. A few years ago I was clearly more concerned about "wide." What could I "produce" with my life? How could I multiply the numbers? A few years later, as a result of some personal maturing in me as well as some prodding by spiritually seasoned colleagues, the emphasis has changed to "deep." As an added bonus, God has shown me a different form of "wide"—the arm of compassion and justice as an inevitable outgrowth of the deepening process.

I have pursued a more authentic discipleship. The search has been rewarding. I rejoice in the growth that God gives. I praise and thank God for it.

Do you hunger for a deeper level of life, for inner renewal, for a connection with the living God? The deepening hunger is contagious! A Christian who goes deeper in both spiritual strength and concern for the world possesses positive, transmittable qualities. And the fruits of the deepening process are contagious outreach to those who have no faith *but wish they did!*

Sing "Deep and Wide" as a child might sing it. Make up your own tune if you need to. Use the gestures (in the shower or in private devotions). Continue to probe deeper. God will give breadth. Let the Spirit of the Living God build a new creation in your soul each day. The fruits of that work of God will generate new hope in those around you.

Prayer: Gracious God, deepen my relationship with you so that my life will be an instrument of witness.

But speaking the truth in love, we must grow up in every way into him who is the head, into Christ.
(Ephesians 4:15)

32. FAST AND EARLY

●●●●●●●●●●●●

One year the emphasis in my favorite garden seed catalogue was highly unsettling. The trend seemed to be toward crops that were "fast and early" in germination and final yield. These were seeds fashioned by the latest seed development of hybrids and new varieties.

The listings included a new "Good 'n Early VFN Hybrid" tomato, a "Rapid Hybrid" cabbage, an "Early Silver Line" melon, a "fast-growing" spinach, and others. So many of the new vegetables seemed to be on the fast track.

Do you suppose that our society's need for immediate results and instant gratification is catching up with the home gardening movement? We seem to crave those things in life that come quickly: fast food, fast service, "instant" potatoes, even "quick" oatmeal for the cholesterol-conscious crowd.

The presumed new push for "fast and early" crops may bring disappointment. Speedy growth is not always a step toward the best nutrition.

God calls us to the urgency of the Kingdom. But God also is very patient. Good growth takes time, careful nurturing, systematic feeding, and adequate root development. Time and careful nurturing are the wisdom of the gospel and mainstay of the Christian discipling.

I'll continue to order those seeds that have proven to be good growers in my home garden. I'll be content with my tomatoes whenever they ripen, even though I admit an eagerness for the first red ripe one to appear. I will continue to enjoy a modest crop of asparagus, which took at least four years to begin to produce shoots for our table.

And I will remember the graciousness of a God who is patient with me and who works with all of us in the slow, careful, purposeful adventures of the Kingdom.

Prayer: God, give me growth, and grant me the patient awareness of that growth day by day.

> *In returning and rest you shall be saved; / in quietness and in trust shall be your strength.*
>
> (Isaiah 30:15)

33. HOT CAPS

●●●●●●●●●●●●●

I purchased several dozen paper hot caps to cover the fragile new greenhouse plants that I was setting into my garden. Danger from freezing or hard frost was past, but other pests mandated special care for a while.

High winds could batter the frail seedlings unduly. Birds could munch on the young, tender leaves—even though there was an abundance of other food available for them. Hard spring downpours of rain could bruise or break the immature stems.

I placed the hot caps carefully over each plant and secured them in place. I cut a small slice in the top to allow appropriate breathing and to prevent the interior temperature from soaring too high on an occasional warm spring day. Green would begin to break through the sliced opening in due course.

When the plants were strong enough, I would remove the hot caps and allow them to continue vigorous growth toward maturity. The right moment would be evident. For the overall health of the plant, I could not wait too long after the moment occurred.

Life is filled with "right moments" when you can say yes to life, to Christ, to faith, and to a direction for the future. In those moments you remove the protective covering and proceed toward the fullness of personhood in Christ that God intends.

Prayer Focus: Ask God to show you which areas of your life require less protection and more courageous growth.

34. DEPLANING INSTRUCTIONS

• • • • • • • • • • • •

I flew into Pittsburgh late one evening. The flight attendant on the plane had been unusually upbeat and enthusiastic with all of his announcements to the passengers. However, it was obvious that his energy began to run down at the end.

He welcomed us to Pittsburgh with the usual speech: "Stay in your seats. Remember that parcels can shift in the overhead compartments. The local time in Pittsburgh is _____."

He concluded with words something like this: "Have a great evening here in Pittsburgh, or wherever your final destination may be. And . . . and . . . have a great day . . . I guess!"

His enthusiasm was depleted.

Human weakness and energy do fail us. Fortunately, we do not rely upon our own resources. God's promise is always ready for our faith appropriation: "For thus said the Lord GOD, the Holy One of Israel: / In returning and rest you shall be saved; / in quietness and in trust shall be your strength (Isaiah 30:15).

Prayer Focus: Try this psalm prayer today: "Turn to me and be gracious to me; / give your strength to your servant" (Psalm 86:16).

> *He gives power to the faint, / and strengthens the powerless.*
>
> (Isaiah 40:29)

35. THE RELENTLESS PURSUIT OF PERFECTION

●●●●●●●●●●●●

A birthday card I received from my grandchildren one year is a classic. The outside reads: "Happy birthday to a grandfather who's kind, intelligent, understanding, patient, and all around wonderful."

When opened, the card says, "In fact, if you owned a pizza parlor, you'd be just about perfect."

Marvelous! As a grandfather, I always can be "going on to perfection." I'm not quite there. Even with a pizza parlor, I'd still be only "just about" perfect. But I can press on.

Years ago, a friend of mine was seriously threatened by the thought of Christ's call to perfection. In fact, he was so badly threatened that he allowed this single matter to stand between him and a vibrant faith. He felt somewhat constrained to reject any serious dialogue with the gospel because he was so sure that perfection was an obstacle and an impossible dream by an idealist named Jesus. Regrettably, he died before I had the opportunity to share my good news with him.

"Perfection" is actually better expressed as "maturity."

Our passion is for maturity. In God's eyes, we approach perfection when we approach maturity. You are invited to grow toward mature personhood in the plan of God.

Maturity does not develop casually or by occasional dabbling. It is the fruit of serious, exciting, disciplined living. That kind of effort is well worth making.

Prayer: Gracious Lord, prod me toward maturity of faith and hope. Let me be "made perfect" by your love.

. . . so that you may be mature and complete, lacking in nothing.

(James 1:4)

---

36. THE MAILBOX

• • • • • • • • • • • •

Our curbside mailbox barely extended above the four-foot snow drifts. The supporting post was almost totally buried. I had to stand on precarious tiptoe and reach across the bank of snow to retrieve two days worth of mail. The ground seemed to radiate a frozen chill as I stretched across the distance to release the fastener.

I pulled a wad of mail out with one hand and closed the door with the other. Instantly, I spotted the advertisement on top of the pile. It was for a new "barefoot grass" lawn service.

There I was reaching across a record-breaking embankment of snow on a record-low-temperature day with my fingers almost frozen to the metal door of the mailbox. And what did I find in my hands? An invitation to turn my lawn into a lush carpet of green! I laughed out loud at the irony of the moment.

No amount of strategic market planning could have predicted that this mailing would arrive when it did. Nevertheless, it spoke of paradox and incongruity.

As I studied the advertisement briefly, I thought of the ways in which the Christian story is an incredible paradox as well. Jesus suffered that we might find strength. Jesus died in order to bring new wholeness to our living.

We are called to sacrifice in order to flourish. It is in dying to selfishness and self-centeredness that we find the abundant life. All of these messages are beyond full comprehension; yet all of them bring the richest measure of hope and celebration to our lives. As one writer suggests, the story of Jesus is the story of "paradox and reversal."

In the midst of whatever holds you down in these days, reach out and retrieve God's paradoxical but powerful Good News. That News affords a dramatic word for your life.

Prayer: Thank you, God, for the paradoxical, the inexplicable, the mystery that is the wonder of your being and your way with us.

For whatever is born of God conquers the world. And this is the victory that conquers the world, our faith.

(1 John 5:4)

37. THE LAUGHTER
OF HOPE

•••••••••••••

On his eightieth birthday, Bob Hope said, "I don't feel eighty. In fact I don't feel anything until about noon. And then it's time for my nap."

Laughter is an integral part of Christian living. One of my favorite pieces of art depicts Jesus with his head thrown back in uproarious laughter.

Stories in the Old Testament are filled with humor. God called Abraham to uproot his entire family and move to a new land when he was seventy-five years old. Moses was called to lead the people of Israel out of captivity when he was eighty years old. Do you see the obvious humor in the stories? Both men were already enjoying their senior-citizen discounts. Both were already collecting social security. God laughs and the story unfolds.

Abraham and Sarah are told that they will become parents in their old age. Abraham is one hundred years old. Sarah is ninety. When the message comes to Abraham, he rolls on the ground with laughter. He laughs so hard that he cannot get enough breath to stand upright. Sarah hears the news from behind the tent flap. She begins to snicker and must cover her mouth to avoid bursting into uproarious laughter. The very idea of her conceiving a child at ninety years of age!

We are part of a tradition in which laughter and humor are important. The psalmist says it well: "Then our mouth was filled with laughter" (126:2*a*). We are permitted, even encouraged, to serve God with mirth.

Prayer Focus: Can you recall some humorous moment in your life when God might have laughed with you? Give thanks for that moment.

> *Happy is everyone who fears the* LORD, */ who walks in his ways.*
>
> (Psalm 128:1)

38. REDISCOVERING SPIRITUALITY

•••••••••••

A sense of God's presence is available to every human being. We see this sense of presence especially in children. Children, however, also tend to grow away from the sense of God's presence as they grow older. In some ways, life is a journey to retouch that spiritual core.

Our oldest son turned thirty recently. He told us about the role of prayer that was reemerging in his life as he wrestled with some large issues. He was "rediscovering his spirituality." He said that it felt good to be in touch with that part of his life again.

Are you growing toward such rediscovery? Jesus said that the kingdom of God is within you. Scholars debate the exact import of that statement in Jesus' teaching. One possible meaning is exactly as it appears: *God is within you! Here and now!*

Prayer Focus: In a brief quiet moment, close your eyes and try to "touch" the presence of God deep within you.

39. DISTRACTIONS

●●●●●●●●●●●●

A woman who lived in Texas often traveled to visit her sister in Hollywood, California. The sister who lived in Texas had always been infatuated with Paul Newman. She never gave up hope that she might catch a glimpse of him on one of her California trips.

During one visit, she walked into an ice cream parlor to purchase a cone. The parlor was small, with a number of stools at a counter. As chance would have it, Paul Newman sat on the very first stool at the counter that night.

The woman was overwhelmed by a combination of awe and awkwardness. She could feel her palms begin to sweat and her knees begin to buckle. Because she did not wish to embarrass herself or be seen as a fool, she politely ordered a cone, paid the clerk, and walked out of the store.

Once outside, she realized that she did not have the cone in her hand. Puzzled—and a bit ruffled—she quickly reentered the store and said to the clerk, "Pardon me. I just purchased a cone from you and paid you, but I did not get my ice cream."

"I don't know what happened, lady," the clerk replied. "I gave you the cone."

"Look," she said with increasing testiness, "do you see an ice cream cone? Young man, I want the cone I paid for."

It was then that Paul Newman spoke up. He said softly, "Lady, you put it in your purse!"

Distractions come easily in this life. Staying focused is not easy. But learning to focus upon who we are, who is around us, and what God might be asking us to do affords the consummate joy of faithful living.

Prayer: God, help me pay attention. Keep me alert and aware. Whom do you want me to speak to today? In what way might what I am about to do glorify you? Keep me focused, please.

Discipline yourselves, keep alert.

(1 Peter 5:8)

40. CONFOUNDING

•••••••••••••

I saw a story about an ad that appeared in the classified section of a large city newspaper. In big, bold letters, it advertised: "Used tombstone for sale." The ad's text read as follows: "Used tombstone for sale. Real bargain to someone named 'Dingo.' For more information, call _____."

Wouldn't you love to know about Dingo? Who was he, and why did he no longer have need for a tombstone?

Much about death and eternal life is a mystery. There is no explanation. The evidence for Easter is strong, but the message and the meaning still confound us. Paul, possibly the strongest believer in the resurrection, wrote of it, "Listen, I will tell you a *mystery!*" (1 Corinthians 15:51, emphasis added).

Jesus is alive. Enough confirming evidence exists to make us doubt our doubts. Yet enough *mystery* persists to keep us growing, searching, and overflowing with wonder.

Perhaps Isaiah best expressed the whole matter in his sixth-century B.C. writing:

For my thoughts are not your thoughts,
    nor are your ways my ways, says the LORD.

For as the heavens are higher than the earth,
    so are my ways higher than your ways
    and my thoughts than your thoughts.
                   (Isaiah 55:8-9)

Prayer: God, grant me restlessness in mystery alongside the certainty of hope.

Blessed be the God and Father of our Lord Jesus Christ! By his great mercy he has given us a new birth into a living hope through the resurrection of Jesus Christ from the dead, and into an inheritance that is imperishable, undefiled, and unfading.

                   (1 Peter 1:3-4)

41. WATCHING AND WAITING

• • • • • • • • • • • •

A man was waiting for a bus to take him from Athens, Georgia, to Greenville, South Carolina. As he purchased his ticket, the agent said, "That bus is running a little late. If you just watch the electronic letter board in the corner, you will know when the bus arrives and it's time to board."

The man wandered the terminal for a while. Eventually he came upon a small machine that said, "For twenty-five cents, this machine will tell you your name, age, city of residence, and something about you."

"That's impossible," the man thought to himself. Nevertheless, he pulled out a quarter and plunked it into the machine. The machine whirred and whistled for a bit and then said, "Your name is Fred Jones. You are thirty-five years old. You live in Athens, Georgia. And you are waiting for a bus to Greenville, South Carolina."

"Incredible!" exclaimed the man. "How does the machine know all of that? I'll bet it cannot do it again." So he plunked another quarter into the slot. Again, the machine whirred and ground for a few moments. Then came the message: "Your name is Fred Jones. You are thirty-five years old. You live in Athens, Georgia. And you are *still* waiting for a bus to Greenville, South Carolina."

"This cannot be happening," said the man. He took off his glasses, mussed his hair a bit, and put up the collar on his jacket. He tried another quarter. The response of the machine was exactly the same: "Your name is Fred Jones. You are thirty-five years old. You live in Athens, Georgia. And you are *still* waiting for a bus to Greenville, South Carolina."

The man glanced across the street and saw a novelty store. He walked out of the bus terminal, crossed the street, and went into the store. There he purchased a pair of glasses with a large nose attached, a wig, a baggy costume shirt, and a cane. He then hobbled back across the street—acting like an elderly, crippled man—and walked up to the machine. He put a fourth quarter into the slot. The machine whirred and groaned, and then said: "Your name is Fred Jones. You are thirty-five years old. You live in Athens, Georgia. And while you were horsing around, you missed the bus to Greenville, South Carolina!"

A parable lies in that story. You and I don't watch and wait very well. We have to be up and doing. Sometimes we are so busy *doing* that we neglect the *watching*. "Watching and waiting" seems trivial when compared to "up and doing." As a result, some of the Good News of Christ passes by almost unnoticed.

Try a little "being" for a change. God is patient, is standing by, and is ready to encourage that dimension of your life.

Prayer Focus: Ask God to give you the capacity to simply "be" with someone today, beyond any official agenda.

42. YOU'RE A TRIP!

•••••••••••

My three-year-old grandson and I were kicking a soccer ball in the backyard. I booted a particularly high ball that landed in the middle of my vegetable garden—something I had strongly encouraged our grandchildren *not* to do!

I smiled and said, "Oh, no, Matthew! The ball's in the middle of the garden. What do we do now?"

Matthew looked at me with a broad smile and said, "Poppa, you're a trip!"

It took me a moment or two to understand what he had said. Then I smiled knowingly. Indeed, I am a "trip." And so are we all.

You are a trip! You are on a trip, an adventure, a journey, a pilgrimage. Perhaps the most significant features in each of these terms are those of movement and progress.

The Christian life is always in motion. You must be still to hear the voice of the One who is our Creator, but that One always calls you to be on the journey. Two of Jesus' most important words in the New Testament were "come" and "go"—both of which are verbs of movement.

You accumulate learning experiences as you live the

Christian life. You are on an adventure of faith that makes you different today than you were five years ago, and you shall be new and different five years from now.

You are a trip. You are *on* a trip. Most important, you travel with a steady Companion. That Companion beckons you on toward a New Creation, toward the fullness of life in which you are forever a "becomer."

Prayer: I give you thanks, O God, for the joy and promise of a wondrous journey with you.

"I hereby command you: Be strong and courageous; do not be frightened or dismayed, for the LORD your God is with you wherever you go."

(Joshua 1:9)

---

43. ENTHUSIASM

●●●●●●●●●●●●

The early disciples of Jesus were transformed into an enthusiastic, fearless crowd. There can be no explanation of their change except the Spirit of God.

Enthusiasm is contagious. The early followers of John Wesley were called "enthusiasts" before they were called "methodists." Enthusiasm is a legacy and promise of the great tradition of the Christian faith. The root meaning of the word *enthusiasm* is "to be in God."

Remember: To discover and rediscover God's gift of enthusiasm is a blessing in your life and a resource for your discipleship.

Prayer Focus: Ask God for fresh enthusiasm throughout this day.

I will greatly rejoice in the LORD, / my whole being shall exult in my God; / for he has clothed me with the garments of salvation, / he has covered me with the robe of righteousness.

(Isaiah 61:10)

---

44. FAN SUPPORT

•••••••••••••

The Pittsburgh Pirates baseball team became the major sports issue for Pittsburgh in recent years. The focus had little to do with sports excellence. Rather, would the Pirates be the *Pittsburgh* Pirates for many more years? Would the team stay in our city? Many complex factors were involved: a buyer for the team, the possibility of a new stadium, sufficient funds to sustain top talent among the players, television contracts (or a lack thereof), and a new labor contact for an extended future.

Another factor, however, could not be ignored: fan support. Unless the fans come through the turnstiles to the games, the team has little reason for being in Pittsburgh or staying for the long term.

The church does not depend upon contracts, a new building, or sustaining top talent. But the church *does* depend upon the presence of growing disciples to ensure long-term ministry and mission. If you or I "sit out" the local gathering events, if we depend upon someone else to keep attendance high, if we attend only when our schedule is convenient, we endanger the health of the church.

I cannot root for the Pittsburgh Pirates to stay in town and never attend a game. I cannot hope that my church will bring viable ministry into the forefront of my community and not attend the "pep rally" and "encouragement session" once every seven days.

Are you a vigorous fan of the Good News in today's setting? Will you be part of a team found faithful to our Covenant God?

Prayer: God, help me to see my presence in worship as more than an obligation or duty. Help me to cheer the Kingdom toward final victory! I *want* to be in that number!

> *All the ends of the earth shall remember / and turn to the LORD; / and all the families of the nations / shall worship before him.*
>
> (Psalm 22:27)

45. CHEERLEADER

• • • • • • • • • • • •

A tourist was walking a strand of the Atlantic beach when a small cluster of people on the ocean's edge drew his attention. As he came closer to the crowd, he realized that a man was about to launch a homemade boat for a solo Atlantic crossing. Bystanders were heckling the would-be adventurer. "You'll never make it," they taunted. "You'll die of thirst. You'll run out of food. The boat will break up in the first storm. You're a fool."

The solitary tourist elbowed his way to the front of the small crowd. With a broad smile and a strong voice, he called to the sailor: "You've got courage, my friend. What an adventure! I admire your spirit. Go in safety and success, and may God go with you."

The world needs strong voices of encouragement. God calls faithful believers to be cheerleaders in the adventure of life. Such a role is not only worthy of God's people; it also enriches the life of the cheerleader.

Prayer Focus: To whom can you provide a word of encouragement and hope today?

> *Therefore encourage one another and build up each other, as indeed you are doing.*
> (1 Thessalonians 5:11)

46. THE U.S. OF @

●●●●●●●●●●●●

Many will recognize the irony of the above title! The "@" is a symbol for a new kind of address. Combined with an appropriate configuration of letters and numbers, the "@" becomes a critical part of an electronic mail address. My own computer "address book" includes several dozen strange-looking configurations that all include "@." And the list is growing.

Meaningful human contact is disappearing. Not only do we not know our next-door neighbors, but we also have fewer human contacts in the workplace. Hundreds of thousands of persons now sit in front of a computer sending "mail" to untold "@" addresses around the world. They enter "chat rooms" and "talk" to faceless (and actually nameless) persons for hours. We *fax* and *e-mail* to an extent unimagined a few years ago. *Pager* messages arc beeper signals across the sky.

In Christ, however, we are names and faces. You are a spiritual being with distinctive spiritual gifts. You have treasure from God in an earthen vessel. You have the unique capacity to look into another's heart, to share an embrace, to touch another in comforting, affirming ways.

I enjoy my e-mail partners. And I will maintain my own e-mail address. But such nomenclature will never be a worthy substitute for authentic human contact. Face-to-face gathering has never been more crucial to our survival and our spiritual well-being.

Prayer: God, enrich my life through personal contact with others. Lead me in at least one new opportunity for such contact today.

47. SEED 'N START

•••••••••••••

A few years ago, my garden seed company initiated a "revised and improved" Seed 'n Start kit. Here was an item that seemed worthy of some consideration.

The catalogue writers called this innovation "unquestionably the best way to start seeds indoors." There would be careful attention to every detail, excellent conditions for early growth, and provision for minimal shock when transplanting to the outside garden. Growing an "increased yield" was virtually guaranteed.

I like to think of the gathering of Christians in worship and in small group ministries as a sort of "seed 'n start" kit for God's mission in the community. As small clusters of people gather, seeds are planted.

The energy of such gatherings has been apparent since the beginnings of Christianity. Are you linked in some fashion to God's best design for "seed 'n start"?

Prayer: Gracious God, give me a "start-up" group with which to gather periodically—one that will sustain and nurture me in more ways than I can currently imagine.

48. ABUNDANCE OF ENOUGH

• • • • • • • • • • • •

A college student maintained an answering machine for his dorm phone. Callers to his room got this message: "Hi, this is Dave. If it's Mom or Dad, please send money. If it's the dry cleaner, I sent the money. If it's the student loan office, you didn't loan me enough money. If it's a friend, you still owe me money. If it's a woman, please leave your name and number and I'll get right back to you. And don't worry. I have plenty of money!"

Not everyone has plenty. But most of us are not poor. We have claimed insufficiency for so long that we now believe it to be true.

Any collective body of Christians in this country has sufficient resources to do whatever God is calling them to do. We may not have met all of our *wants*. But we have few real financial *needs*.

Most of us have an abundance of enough.

Prayer: God, grant me a deep contentment with enough. Help me see that I truly am blessed with an abundance of enough in my life.

And my God will fully satisfy every need of yours according to his riches in glory in Christ Jesus.
(Philippians 4:19)

49. SLAM DUNK!

• • • • • • • • • • • • •

The NBA and NCAA college basketball have made the "slam dunk" a major goal of athletes and a thing of beauty to watch from the sidelines. Not to be outdone by the big guns, my son-in-law has set up a basketball hoop in our grandsons' bedroom.

Naturally, the hoop is not very high. And the basketball is the Nerf variety. (Mother insists!) But "slam dunk" is the most sought-after feat in every round of bedroom basketball.

Father simply tosses the ball from a prone position on the floor—so as not to give himself undue advantage. The seven-year-old charges the hoop and sinks a few good shots. The five-year-old has to charge the basket a bit harder, but he has amazing coordination for his age and size. The two-year-old, never to be left out of any competition, stands on a small table and ceremoniously slam dunks with every possession of the ball! Each member of the family is participating, albeit at different levels.

So it is with the remarkable journey of the Christian faith. Each of us engages the challenges of the Christian walk at a different level. You may flounder a bit because you are an inexperienced player. You may score an occasional slam dunk as you seek to build a margin of faith that will sustain you for the long haul. At times you may need special assistance because it is the only way you can reach the goal.

The goal of the Christian life, however, is not a "slam dunk." The goal is simply to play the game, to engage life with enthusiasm and confidence, looking regularly to the Master Coach for counsel and encouragement. How well we understand or comprehend so much mystery does not finally matter—so long as we do not allow ourselves to be only on the sidelines, watching!

Prayer: Gracious God, help me to develop and grow in the challenge of faithful Christian living.

50. IN SEARCH OF EXCELLENCE

• • • • • • • • • • • •

Excellence honors God. God is praised through excellent participation in the gathering of God's people, excellent devotional disciplines, excellent compassion toward one another, and excellent commitment to what is just and right. Not lavish, not demonstrably showy, not haughty, but excellent.

The Bible also teaches excellence in generosity. God is praised, and the church is alive when God's people give in an excelling fashion.

Does your giving honor God? Does your offering say something positive about your relationship with the Almighty? To "excel" is to rise above, to surpass expectations. To excel in giving is to be outstanding, to eclipse the status quo. Paul reminds us: "Now as you excel in everything—in faith, in speech, in knowledge, in utmost eagerness, and in our love for you—so we want you to excel also in this generous undertaking" (2 Corinthians 8:7).

Giving reflects the central core of our lives—Who is in charge and how much that authority really matters. Someone has said that excellence is not being perfect but doing the best you can with what you have. Now *that* is an encouraging word!

Prayer Focus: Ask God to give you an "eager excellence" in your giving decisions.

> *Therefore, my beloved, be steadfast, immovable, always excelling in the work of the Lord, because you know that in the Lord your labor is not in vain.*
>
> (1 Corinthians 15:58)

51. SUBSTANTIVE GIVING

●●●●●●●●●●●●

The story about the widow's gifts at the temple treasury is certainly about giving, but it is a message about much more as well. Here is the story of adventure with God. Giving as a disciple of Jesus is about that same adventure.

The journey of the Christian life is not an easy one. It is not necessarily smooth or prosperous or financially successful. But that journey is always an adventure. Part of the adventure is giving.

The amount of your gift is not as important as the cost to you. Jesus is talking about risks in giving and in living. Jesus is calling for an almost recklessly adventurous spirit.

Some gave to the temple treasury out of abundance. One woman gave out of her substance. Jesus watched her for a moment and then said to his disciples, in effect, Take note of what is happening here. It's important. "All of them have contributed out of their abundance, but she out of her [substance]" (Luke 21:4).

Does your giving have the sound of "substance"?

Prayer: God, grant me to give offerings out of my substance. Teach me what that means for me.

I will thank you in the great congregation; / in the mighty throng I will praise you.

(Psalm 35:18)

52. BETWEEN SOUND AND LIGHT

●●●●●●●●●●●●

The evening was perfect for a walk on the beach. Darkness was falling fast, but there seemed to be ample time. The Carolina seashore in April was most pleasant—calm and cool. Spring had arrived weeks earlier. I walked briskly for thirty minutes in the evening twilight. Upon turning to head back, it became apparent that it would be dark before I could return to the house.

Darkness quickly enveloped me as I retraced my steps along the beach. A few stars were out, but there was no moon this night. The occasion caught me off guard. An initial uncertainty came upon me.

Gradually, however, my mind began to sense a parable in this unexpected setting. As I walked the extraordinary wide expanse of sand at night at low tide, there were only two indicators to guide me. One was the sound of the ocean on my right. The steady pounding of the surf was clear evidence of one boundary. The other indicator was the uneven line of scattered dim lights in the beach-front homes about seventy-five yards to my left. These lights did not illuminate any portion of the beach. They only provided a compass point to keep me more or less on course.

Visibility was near zero. The only way to navigate was to continue walking between the steady sounds of the ocean breakers and the irregular lights from those homes.

There are times in the walk of faith when we can no longer see the path beneath our feet. There are times when we find ourselves in almost total darkness. Such times mean the use of new senses. In particular, such times call for a spiritual sense that is greater than that which the human eye can see.

God has not promised you a clear and brightly lit path at all times. But God has promised you strength and help to make it through any darkness. God has promised a light in Jesus Christ that no darkness can ever overcome. Such light is the gift and blessing of a gracious God. And that blessing is sufficient to your deepest need.

Prayer: God, grant me sufficient awareness of your voice and your light to guide me forward.

For we walk by faith, not by sight.
                              (2 Corinthians 5:7)

53. APPLAUSE! APPLAUSE!

●●●●●●●●●●●●

How we love to cheer and applaud a great performance: a beautiful reception by one of football's great wide receivers, a stirring performance by a great symphony or opera company, a dramatic portrayal by a great actor, years of faithful and talented service by a co-worker in our company, moments of standing ovations shared over a lifetime.

One of the first gestures a small child learns is applause. The face lights up, the tiny hands reach into the air, and enthusiastic, somewhat uncoordinated applause dominates the child's whole being. How I have cherished the spontaneous applause in each of our grandchildren in the earliest years of their lives. Almost every young child in my congregation loves to give me a "high five." To applaud in the face of wonder or appreciation is natural and genuine to human nature.

Scripture reminds us of the majestic performance of God on our behalf: the gift of life; the special joys of family ties and significant friendships; the mysterious and delicate harmony of creation; the durability of the Christian church; the incredible gift of amazing grace.

Sometimes we are moved to assess the beauty of the night sky or to review the people and events of a given day or to realize anew the joy and promise of God's steadfast love, and we want to applaud the Creator—in spirit if not in actuality. Like a trusting child, we clap our hands in joyful appreciation.

We so need a few moments on a regular basis to enter into the great human experience of praise. It is a way of life for the Christian. God has made us. We belong! O be joyful in the Lord, all you people. Enter the sacred Presence with thanksgiving! (*See* Psalms 95:2 and 100:2.) Applause! Applause!

Prayer Focus: Stop for a moment, clasp your hands together, and silently affirm God for some specific goodness in your life today. If you are alone, try applause!

Rejoice in the LORD, *O you righteous. / Praise befits the upright.*

(Psalm 33:1)

---

54. PORCH SITTING

●●●●●●●●●●●●

Living in the suburbs has meant the demise of one of life's finer arts: porch sitting. Throughout much of the nation's rural areas and small towns, porch sitting is still priceless summer treasure. Suburbanites such as myself, however, do not even have porches.

We sometimes have decks, many of which are designated primarily for cooking and eating. We cook, eat, and then go back to work or into air-conditioned comfort to watch television. Precious few hours are actually spent in ordinary "deck sitting." Whereas porches were usually designed to face the street and watch the neighborhood, decks are mostly toward the back of the house in secluded privacy.

I remember classic porch sitting from my childhood visits with my maternal grandparents on a farm in Tennessee. I would sit for hours with my grandfather, and, while close in proximity, we seldom found it necessary to speak.

Peripheral activities related to porch sitting are numerous. One can read or watch squirrels trying to get into a bird feeder. One can enjoy the curiosity and laughter of children chasing lightning bugs.

Sometimes porch sitting includes rambling, adult

conversation. Reminiscing is a favorite "agenda" of porch sitters, especially among families. Sometimes there is opportunity to watch people nearby, including other porch sitters. But sometimes the moments are just for being still without any agenda.

Sometime soon, find a porch and sit for a while. If you don't have a porch—and can't build one—borrow one! Any life that is devoid of porch sitting is a life that is too full and complex.

I don't know who invented porches, but I believe God inspired something of the invention! Porch sitting is therapeutic, healing, and genuinely human. It is part of how life is meant to be.

Prayer: God, help me to find a porch today—in reality or in my mind's eye. And, God, make those moments quality time!

Be still before the LORD, *and wait patiently for him.*
(Psalm 37:7)

---

55. YOU CAN'T FOOL MOTHER NATURE!

•••••••••••••

Early May brought unusually warm weather. The planting instructions on the box of corn seed said, "Plant after all danger of frost, and after the ground is thoroughly warm." I decided to chance it. Early corn would be wonderful. I lost! The ground was too cold. The seed rotted in the furrows before it could germinate.

Two weeks later it was warm again. The new box of corn seed said, "Earliest possible planting date: May 15." I tried again on May 15. I wanted that early corn. I lost again! It was too early. The ground was still too cold and wet for the sensitive corn seeds to germinate.

Ten days later I was ready for round three. (It was going to be an expensive year for corn!) But the experts were right. One cannot rush the delicate balance of necessary weather patterns and soil preparation for sweet corn.

Human life is very much within that delicate balance of nature. We are neither above nature nor beyond nature. We are interwoven in nature. The marvelous and creative gift of human life is to be valued as part of creation itself. Know your strengths and your weaknesses. Know the rules for maximum quality of life. Know that God wants maximum bodily health through you for as long as life endures.

Prayer: God, help me to care for this bodily system, this "clay pot," this earthen vessel that you have made and given.

But we have this treasure in clay jars, so that it may be made clear that this extraordinary power belongs to God and does not come from us.

(2 Corinthians 4:7)

---

56. CHAPEL IN THE HILLSIDE

• • • • • • • • • • • •

Sedona, Arizona, is an exquisite setting for a day-long trip north of Phoenix. The sculptured red hills and shafts of rock are stunningly beautiful. Nothing in my native state of Pennsylvania comes even close in resemblance to Sedona.

Naturally, the town is a tourist attraction. Hundreds of tourists arrive in Sedona each week—especially in the delightful climate of "winter" in the desert southwest. Shops abound, from authentic Native American crafts to the requisite fudge. One can purchase almost anything in Sedona, Arizona.

I was not prepared, however, for one special site on the south side of the town. A generous and spiritually energized benefactor placed a beautiful chapel on the side of the mountain that overlooks the town. The chapel is open all day, and Gregorian chant music plays softly in the background.

What a contrast! And what a beautiful serendipitous mix: to gaze upon nature's red rock beauty from a chapel setting while listening to the medieval chants of the church!

We need to see more of life this way—to see God's

creative masterpiece from a special vantage point with sacred music playing softly. What a marvelous way to look at life.

Try it! Find a piece of creation's beauty in the next few days. (You may not have to go very far, actually!) Carry with you some form of music that speaks to your own soul. Let the grace of God flow over you. Allow yourself some time for sacred nurture. You deserve it and you need it!

Prayer Focus: Ask God to lead you toward the time and the place for some reflection in the midst of creation's indigenous beauty.

> *The heavens are telling the glory of God; / and the firmament proclaims his handiwork.*
>
> (Psalm 19:1)

57. DON'T MISS THE GOOD NEWS!

•••••••••••••

Three-year-old granddaughter Casey stepped up to the miniature golf check-in point. She eagerly pointed to the club and the ball she wanted. "How old are you?" asked the man in charge.

"I'm fwee," came the reply.

"Then you are free!" he said to her with great kindness.

"No, I'm fwee!" she insisted, with a puzzled expression.

"She means she's three years old." I spoke up for her.

"I know what she means," said the man with a revealing smile. "And I am telling you that since she's three, she's free! She doesn't have to pay to play the game."

Casey almost missed the good news.

Are you so preoccupied with your own agenda that you miss what God is trying to say to you? Do you ever insist on some personal schedule before God, failing to hear the gentle, heartening message of Jesus?

God's word to us is always Good News! Whether it comes in the quiet stillness of a small inward voice, in the majestic anthem of a choir, in deep reflection upon a series of connected experiences, in a turn of phrase, or in an illustration in a sermon, God's voice is the voice of good news.

One of the most important lessons of the Christian life is that of learning to listen to the Spirit, to hear God's input. Many spiritual teachers say that discernment is the difficult discipline. Perhaps! But first you listen, become attuned, and hear the basic message in what God would say to you.

The very first thing God wishes to say is clearly this: "You are loved. You are valued. You are important." God sent Jesus to make that good news very clear.

Hear that initial good news now. Stop the hectic race for a short while. Stop the extraneous conversation. Listen! Don't miss the good news that is so fundamental to a whole and contented life.

And remember: That good news is free, no matter what your age!

Prayer Focus: Extend your cupped hands forward in prayer. Ask God to fill your "cup" with the good news that you are loved, valued, and cherished. Let the Heart of the universe speak to your heart!

He destined us for adoption as his children through Jesus Christ, according to the good pleasure of his will, to the praise of his glorious grace that he freely bestowed on us in the Beloved.

(Ephesians 1:5-6)

---

58. DON'T LEAVE IT TO CHANCE!

•••••••••••••

Who taught you how to use the Bible? Who gave you your first instructions on prayer? Who explained to you the meaning of a worship service? Where did you first learn the importance of "loving your neighbor" or of "doing what is right" in the eyes of God? Where did you learn discipleship?

Many of us learned at the knees of a beloved grandparent or parent. Some of us learned in Sunday school. A few of us learned because someone lovingly took the time to mentor us along the way. A minuscule number learned on our own—without much help or encouragement from anyone.

Today, disciples are an endangered species. Would-be followers of the Master do not find the going easy in the midst of secular lifestyles and consumptive ways. We have few guidelines and instructions—and fewer models to give us encouragement, to prod us onward to the "higher ground."

Listen to the still, small voice of God. If that Voice calls you to discipleship, do not resist. Do not leave your Christian walk with the Master to chance any longer.

Prayer Focus: Breathe a prayer of thanks to God for someone who has nurtured you as a Christian—whether in your childhood or youth or adulthood. Ask God to grant you a new mentor for the living of these days.

59. ADD SOME GLITTER!

•••••••••••

I watched her closely from inside the family room of our home. She stood proudly on the deck with a bit of Christmas tinsel in her beak. She had the look of triumph about her, as though she had just discovered buried treasure.

In a way, she had! This enterprising mother robin had located several pieces of tinsel from the area where we had dragged our fading Christmas tree out of the house for curbside disposal several months earlier. The nest for her young this year would be no ordinary nest. It would have twigs and leaves and other natural elements, to be sure. But it also would have the glitter of bits of tinsel which she had found.

I have no idea how many pieces she found or how many times she returned. She made several trips to the same spot for more tinsel.

Surely God rejoices when we discover that special "tinsel" that makes the celebration of faith more beautiful before him and more engaging to others. The Christian walk is a simple walk of faith, hope, and obedience to the Risen Christ. But when a bit of glitter is added from time to time, whether serendipitously or deliberately planned, the walk becomes more attractive, and the heart of God is glad.

Prayer Focus: You are made in the image of God. Ask God to assist you in adding some "glitter" to the image you reflect around you today.

Let your light shine before others, so that they may see your good works and give glory to your Father in heaven.

(Matthew 5:16)

---

60. WELL-CENTERED

•••••••••••••

Our daughter and her family had just moved into a new home in Virginia. The home included a wonderful front porch facing the yard and street. She returned from shopping one afternoon to present me with a four-foot-wide porch swing to be placed on the five-foot-wide porch. I was asked to install the swing.

I immediately saw some fringe benefits in complying with her request. Having just been blessed with a new granddaughter, I could sit on the swing and hold her in my arms in the early evening and cherish some private bonding time.

Given that foreseen opportunity, I needed to make doubly certain that this swing was securely and correctly installed. That meant I needed to find the beams within the porch roof overhead. I must secure the heavy-duty eye-screws in the exact center of those beams. Without placement in the center, the screws could gradually work loose or crack the outer edges of the supporting members. My carpentry skills being minimal, I spent most of an afternoon getting the swing correctly installed. Finding the center of hidden beams was not an easy process.

Later that evening, I sat on the swing holding my

two-week-old granddaughter in my arms. I sang to her softly, occasionally glancing up at the large screws I had secured to the ceiling beams overhead.

The centering of your life is of consummate importance. Such centering needs to happen as early in the life journey as possible. There is only one enduring Center, and his name is Jesus. He is the nucleus, the pivotal point, the meaning, and the end of our lives. He is the stay and support in storm and tempest. He is Life itself.

Prayer Focus: Breathe a prayer of thanks to God for the One who gives your life a center and a focus today.

Christ is all and in all!

(Colossians 3:11)

61. FEEDING
THE DUCKS

●●●●●●●●●●●●

One of the exciting traditions for this grandfather and his grandchildren is the feeding of ducks. Wherever ducks are to be found, they are to be fed. It's axiomatic.

A recent sequence of duck feedings, however, brought an unexpected development. The sequence came near a pond in Williamsburg, Virginia, and unfolded over three days. We had one loaf of (duck cheap) white bread, which was divided into thirds for each of the three trips to the pond. I walked with my grandsons, ages four and two, from our apartment to the pond area for the anticipated feeding. They carried the bread, and I navigated the expedition.

The first day, the ducks came slowly, even reluctantly. They were not too sure about these two noisy little people and the tall one who accompanied them. Once reassured, however, they ate gladly of the broken bits of bread that were thrown in front of them.

The second trip, two days later, a few of the ducks thought they might recognize the three familiar forms on the horizon. Those few came quickly to feed, and the others quickly got the message and joined them.

The third trip, at the end of the week, was astounding. When we were still a long way off, the ducks saw us coming—a tall human figure with a much shorter one on either side, all walking toward the pond. With considerable fanfare and loud quacking, they began racing toward us at breakneck (duck waddle) speed. It was as though one of them had said, "Hey, you guys! Here come those three humans again with bread." I had never seen a duck race before. I also understood the momentary terror on the faces of two little boys. But the ducks knew exactly why we were coming. They were counting on our bread!

Hunger remains a major issue on planet earth. We in the West do not have the rampant starvation of some Third World countries, yet hunger is real here as well.

Many who are hungry count upon God's more privileged people to be catalysts and workers on behalf of adequate supplies and distribution of bread. Hurting nations have learned to expect a great deal from the exceptionally benevolent arm of Christ's people. The hungry, ailing, cold, and shelterless poor hope the tradition will endure. God is hoping also.

Prayer Focus: Ask God to lead you to one intentional act of compassion for a hungry or hurting person in the next few days. Then give thanks for the spirit of Jesus in that call.

> *"Come, you that are blessed by my Father, inherit the kingdom prepared for you from the foundation of the world; for I was hungry and you gave me food."*
> (Matthew 25:34-35a)

62. THE GREAT WALK

•••••••••••••

The morning was damp and chilly. A heavy, misty fog had fallen over the mountain. All was quiet and peaceful. A short hike before breakfast seemed inviting.

As I walked along a wide trail, I enjoyed a few of nature's wonders. Two deer stood sentinel at a distance, ears forward, alerted by some unfamiliar noise, perhaps my passing. Multiple varieties of birds moved playfully along the ground and flew among the branches in the trees overhead. One small field was covered entirely with a thick moss, and leaves from the previous fall were on the ground. Some remaining color added special interest to my morning journey. I was wandering in the quiet beauty of nature at peace.

About a quarter of a mile from my starting point, I came upon a small, carefully painted sign leaning against a tree. It read:

Columcile's Woodland Care
and
Ecological Conservation Project
No wood cutting or hunting!
Hiking celebrated

The sign gave me fresh motivation. I moved with a new lightness of step.

Another hundred feet, a fork in the path to the right, an arrow indicating the direction, another sign. This one read quite simply:

The Great Walk

Two signs in the woods; one marvelous invitation! The life of faith is a celebrated great walk. It is a serendipitous adventure amidst the wonders of God's creative grace. Even on days that are overcast, cloudy, chilly, or uncomfortably wet, it is still a great walk!

Hiking celebrated! The great walk! What remarkable phrases set before an early-morning walker on a mountainside. What powerful phrases to encourage you and me on the journey through this life. We step out and walk by faith. We celebrate the journey. We are sustained by grace. Thanks be to God for the great walk.

Prayer: Dear God, lighten my step and freshen my outlook this day. Help me to have a great walk with you.

63. ERNIE

•••••••••••••

Our first grandson was starting to talk. He was eighteen months old, and the words flowed in a never-ending stream of proud mimicry and pieces of adult sentences. In the process, he had begun to fix upon names for his grandparents. Through a series of silly prodding and teasing events one afternoon, his grandmother became "Ernie"—as in the famous Bert and Ernie duo on Sesame Street. The name has affectionately stuck with all subsequent grandchildren! Even a few friends have picked it up!

We all tend to develop a series of affectionate names for caring, loving persons in our lives. You probably have one or two extended family members with a distinctively different name that endears you to them, or to your memory.

Much is being written today about the appropriate name for God. Should God's name be "Father" or "Abba" or "Lord" or "Sovereign One" or simply "Love"? Shall we designate God as "Friend" or "Parent" or "Holy Other" or "Ground of all Being"?

Does God care what name you use in personal prayer? Are you supposed to exercise great care in the name applied in this most vital and intimate of all relationships? Must you hesitate to name the sacred Name until we have carefully assessed theological propriety?

I offer this suggestion. Let each of us, as a child of God, find our own term of endearment, perhaps as Jesus did centuries ago. In the privacy of personal prayer, we will not stand judged by our fumbling for correct language or other proper forms of address. Rather, we shall be received according to our growing trust and confidence in the One who longs to draw us ever closer in love.

Prayer Focus: By what name do you most often address God? Might you use an alternate name occasionally? Speak to God right now! Simply name God's name. Then say this: "_____, I ask only that you be a sacred presence in my soul."

Therefore God also highly exalted him / and gave him the name / that is above every name, / so that at the name of Jesus / every knee should bend.
(Philippians 2:9-10*a*)

64. SMALL-SCALE SOIL EROSION

• • • • • • • • • • • •

The backyard of our Pittsburgh home lies reasonably flat. However, in Western Pennsylvania, any "flatness" is somewhat relative. Actually, my yard does tip slightly from east to west.

Aggravations with my plot of garden soil have been minimal. I take care of the soil, replenish it faithfully each growing season, and cultivate it carefully. However, over the years I have had one nagging problem. The soil seems somewhat less abundant at the eastern end, and somewhat more abundant on the west. There is a slight "recession" in the soil line at the east, and a slight "hump" at the west. Every couple of years, I have taken several wheelbarrow loads from west to east, but the problem has not disappeared.

It took some time for me to realize that the cause of this phenomenon is soil erosion. Because there is a slight slope, the top soil is gradually shifting from east to west.

Something similar can easily happen to each of us in this time in history. Slowly, quietly, the secularization of life may erode some part of the sacred from the precious soil of our souls. The accumulation of gadgets to make life easier; the proliferation of weekend getaways; the attempts to get to our bank accounts with long-term membership payments to health spas, vacation packages, and full-season sports packages; and the endless growth of television channels from which to choose erodes the sacred and accentuates the secular.

For the most part, the secular is not an evil. Perhaps that is why it is such a potential threat. It creeps slowly over our lives, snatching precious moments once used for reading, spending time with our children, talking with our spouses, or even worshiping God.

Unless we make every effort to regain some of that precious topsoil of the spirit, we may find ourselves depleted and deprived of that which gives this human journey meaning and depth.

Agricultural experts warn us of the dangers of soil erosion in the great crop-raising belts of America. I experience a bit of that danger in my own backyard. But even more important, I experience it in the depths of my own soul.

Secular erosion is powerful. But regular communion with God's Spirit is a suitable deterrent.

Prayer: God, give me a steadfastness toward you and that which you value in and through me. Give me a watchful eye toward any "soul erosion" in my own life.

Finally, be strong in the Lord and in the strength of his power. Put on the whole armor of God, so that you may be able to stand.

(Ephesians 6:10-11)

65. FOLLOWING

•••••••••••••

At nineteen months of age, our youngest grandson spoke only a few intelligible words. But he had a distinct way of making his wishes known.

His tactic was systematic. He called me out of my reading chair with a captivating smile and a few grunts of insistence. Next, he took a few steps in a given direction, quickly turning to see if I were following. If I were at all hesitant, he reached up, grabbed as many of my fingers as his little hand would hold, and pulled me toward an unknown destination.

Jesus does something very similar. He calls you to follow him. You may be hesitant or reluctant at first. But his positive smile and spirit of encouragement are contagious. You choose to follow. You are not always sure where he is taking you. And even when you "arrive," you may not always be sure where you are.

Such is the way it *always* will be for the Christian pilgrim. We know the One whom we follow. Although initially hesitant, we know we eventually must accede to his persuasive invitation. Sometimes we know where he leads. Other times we barely comprehend what his beckoning certainty is all about. We go simply because of the One who calls.

Today is the day to heed the persistent call. Jesus' invitation extends to each of us more often than we realize. We follow into the occasional unknown, trusting that his leadership always will be life-giving and durable.

Prayer: "O give me grace to follow, my Master and my Friend!" (from "O Jesus, I Have Promised," by John E. Bode, 1866).

66. IN PRAISE OF PLAY

•••••••••••••

I joined our children at a water slide playground near the beach. I picked up a small, gray mat, and looked skeptically toward the long climb to the top. Children and youth scurried past me on the paved path. Even the very youngest of the children seemed much more eager and excited than I was.

Upon reaching the top, I was faced with one of three choices. Three options for my first ride! Which slide was the least dangerous? Least threatening? Least potentially bone bruising? Since the line had to keep moving, I timidly picked the entry to my right. I sat down on the mat amidst a small stream of water in a narrow, slick, green channel. I pushed off. Instantly, I found myself hurtling with frightening speed down what proved to be the steepest channel of the gigantic water slide.

Would it ever end? Would I come to a merciful end? I forgot one clear instruction that read, "Hold elbows close to your body." As a result, my elbows felt as though they were being rubbed raw. (Elbows were not designed to be used as body brakes on a water slide!) There was a sudden drop—not unlike those of an occasional sled or toboggan run in the snow—and my bones compacted ever so slightly. Finally, I plowed into the water basin at the end of the slide.

"How was it?" It was my wife calling me from her much safer perch in an observation deck twenty feet overhead.

"I'm not sure," I lied. Then, turning, I started the long climb to do the same foolishness over again. I actually had enjoyed the ride!

Someone has written that play has the spirit of adventure. Play brings peace and delight. We do not play very often. Indeed, our lives are dominated by the conflict between play and work.

Play has a healing and spiritually restorative dimension. Leave some room for play in your life. Let others help you play. (Children and grandchildren are enormously effective in this regard!) Praise God with play. If not a water slide, then a table game or a round of miniature golf.

God surely must have a sense of humor. I know. I sensed something of divine laughter as I careened down that water slide during thirty minutes of modified childhood glee.

Prayer: Dear God, help me to praise you with some form of play, or even playfulness, this day. Help me to live in some praise of play.

He will yet fill your mouth with laughter, / and your lips with shouts of joy.

(Job 8:21)

67. LOVE LIFTED ME

•••••••••••

One of my favorite pictures of our youngest grandson captures an extraordinary moment between him and me. He has crawled toward me in anticipation of some grandfatherly attention. About three feet away, he ceases crawling, brings his arms and upper body upright, rests on his knees, and extends his arms for the expected response: I will pick him up and carry him for a while.

No words are spoken. No sounds of any sort are uttered. He simply extends his arms in confident expectation because he knows that I will not fail to respond. The eyes, arms, the facial expression say it all.

The heart of the Christmas story is one of God reaching out to those who wait with eager longing. The true nature of God is to lift us. All God asks of us is some gesture of faith—some little sign that we know we need God!

Imagine yourself on your knees right now. Ask God to lift you—out of any secular dependency, out of any empty allegiance to material things, out of a plethora of meaningless addictions, out of any trivial pursuits. Ask God to hold you in the sure and certain hope that faith is meant to bring.

Know the promise of One who lifts you—faithfully and securely each day of your life journey.

Prayer Focus: Reread and live the suggestion made two paragraphs above.

> *I will bless you as long as I live; / I will lift up my hands and call on your name.*
>
> (Psalm 63:4)

68. TRACING IMAGES

• • • • • • • • • • • •

I arranged for a wood worker "engineer" to create a special gift for our six-year-old grandson. My friend made a wooden box with piece of plexiglass on the top side and a small electric light bulb inside. Using this box, a child can trace pictures from books or magazines.

I watched my grandson meticulously trace a picture of himself and his younger brother and sister from a current photograph. He got all of the lines just right and then began to color the faces and the clothing to match the picture. The end result was a remarkable achievement for a child of his age. The likeness of final rendering to the original photograph was amazing.

You and I are called to image the presence of Jesus in the world. We are *made* in the image of God to *be* the image of Jesus Christ. Reflecting and sustaining that image is always a gift of grace—not a mere human achievement. But it does require some intentionality on our part.

Jesus invites you to image God's presence in the world. God's call? To be at least a rough tracing of the Master before those whose lives we touch.

Prayer: God, allow me to image something of you before the people I see this day. Help me remember who I am and whom others are to see in me.

69. THE PENDULUM CLOCK

●●●●●●●●●●●●

In the entry hall of our home stands a grandfather clock. The beautiful clock is a family treasure purchased in memory of my father. With precision and resonance, this great clock chimes each quarter of the hour and then "bongs" the appropriate hour of the day or night.

The mechanism within the clock allows us to change the chiming whenever we so choose. Supposedly, such changes add variety and keep the sound from being banished into common familiarity.

The fact is, however, we hardly hear the clock. Only occasionally are we aware of the chiming of the hour. Though the clock must be placed on "silent" to respect the sleep needs of occasional house guests, we who live in the home scarcely hear the various sounds.

Too often, the same is true of the Good News of faith. The sounds, sights, and movements of a Christian witness and lifestyle are reasonably familiar to our daily living. As a result, we may not notice the beauty and majesty of each occasion.

Of special concern are those who are reaching out, who are almost desperate for some connection with God.

We may be so lulled by the familiar, so self-absorbed in our own comfortable places, that we do not hear the questions or see the puzzled looks of those for whom the sounds and sights of our faith are remote, even strange.

We simply cannot allow ourselves to be lulled into dullness and inattentiveness. Heightened sensitivity to those who are searching or who have never heard the Good News is a vital piece of faithful response to that Good News. The constant freshness in the adventure of the Christian life must not be lost. Each disciple is called to alert attention on the journey.

Make phone contact with a new or searching Christian whom you know today!

Prayer: God, grant me today sufficient awareness of someone who is beginning a search for you, or someone who is desperate for some assurance that he or she matters to you. Help me to see several persons with new eyes today.

70. A SPRING NESTING RITUAL

●●●●●●●●●●●●

Ms. Robin had built her nest in a small pine tree adjacent to the deck in our backyard. The tree was destined for removal later that same season because of its badly mis-shaped growth, but it received a reprieve due to its role as a temporary shelter for a homeless robin family.

Unfortunately, I became a major problem for Ms. Robin. The nest was only about ten feet from the sliding door to the deck. Each time I opened that door to cook on the grill or to work in the yard or to read in a deck chair, she scurried from her nest, perched on the post of the split-rail fence, and chirped her annoyance at me with considerable vigor. "Don't you dare disturb my babies," she seemed to shout.

Soon she had three young ones in the nest with mouths wide open. She was almost never at home during the day, for she had a mission to find food for a very hungry brood. I watched her pull worms from the garden soil, circle the scruffy pine tree with a wary eye as to my whereabouts, enter to feed one of her young, and quickly exit in pursuit of another portion of the meal. I may have altered her style a bit, but I never dissuaded her from her carefully designed mission of life.

Her determination is a worthy model for our discipleship. God calls us to a single-minded devotion on the path of discipleship. There may be occasions of diversion. There may be hidden dangers that require the summoning of great courage. Yet the mission of the gospel, the work of the Kingdom, is absolutely essential. We are called to faithfulness in telling the Good News, in caring for those who cannot care for themselves, in feeding the hungry, in holding up a prophetic word to our time, and in maintaining a steadfast vision.

Our mission—to paraphrase one Christian philosopher—is simply "to will one thing"(from the title of Søren Kierkegaard's *Purity of Heart Is to Will One Thing*).

Prayer: Gracious God, by your grace, keep me purposeful, steadfast, and immovable. Let no lesser diversion deter me today or ever.

We have this hope, a sure and steadfast anchor of the soul.

(Hebrews 6:19)

71. A TABLE PREPARED

•••••••••••••

In mid-February our daughter prepared an elegant Valentine's Day breakfast for our grandchildren. It was breakfast in red and white! The feast began with a bowl of fresh strawberries topped with whipped cream. Next came heart-shaped French toast topped with strawberry syrup. Finally, there was strawberry-flavored (and colored) milk in graceful stemware glasses. (The stemware glasses were a nice touch, but a little overboard, I thought!)

As grandparents, we watched in wonder and amazement at this outpouring of love and creativity. While the children offered a few exclamations of appreciation for all of this festive and tasty flair, there were no audible rave reviews.

God sets a bountifully prepared table before you and me. The table is filled with immeasurable divine benevolence. We are children of the cross and the Resurrection. The gift of amazing grace is our legacy, born out of love. The power and promise of this banquet is beyond our capacity to understand.

Occasionally, we remember to give thanks. There are far too few rave reviews. Yet God keeps on giving. In the midst of a life that can be harsh and prickly, God continues to give in love. God gives in excessive abundance. God gives simply because of an incredible depth of caring about who you are and what your life finally means.

"Taste and see," says the psalmist, "that the LORD is good" (Psalm 34:8). Taste and see, indeed!

Prayer Focus: Pick up a scrap of paper and start a list of God's bounty. At some point later today, read over the list and breathe a prayer of great thanksgiving. Close your eyes and say with the psalmist, "O taste and see that the LORD is good" (Psalm 34:8).

72. FULL SERVANTHOOD

•••••••••••••

I pulled into a gas station on an early summer morning in Toms River, New Jersey. The station was much like others I had visited many times, except for an unexpected oddity: All of the pumps said "full"; none said "self." I was puzzled. I always pump my own gas. Momentarily immobilized, I stopped by one pump to search for some instructions. Instantly, a man was at my window to serve me.

This was a full-service gasoline station! Every station in town was a full-service facility. Then I learned something I did not know: Every service station in the state of New Jersey is full service. It's the law!

They pumped my gas. They washed my windows. They checked the oil. They accepted my credit card and brought the receipt to me to sign. The service came with a smile and a "thank you." And the price of a gallon of fuel was at least two cents less than I had last paid at home.

Jesus calls you and claims you for service. Jesus came among us as one who "serves." Jesus' followers can do no less. When you find your place in the servant ministry of Jesus, you find a place of full participation in the best that life offers. To serve another will often feel contrary to the prevailing mood of this modern age. But to serve another will stretch and strengthen your discipleship journey. To serve another will ensure a powerful witness to the one who is Master of your life!

Prayer Focus: In the name of Jesus, find a person or place to be a servant today. Ask God to lead you to that moment and opportunity. Seek the chance to serve. Don't just wait for the occasion to appear. Pray about it now; then move into the remainder of the day in expectation.

> *"The greatest among you will be your servant. All who exalt themselves will be humbled, and all who humble themselves will be exalted."*
> (Matthew 23:11-12)

73. A HOPEFUL SIGN

● ● ● ● ● ● ● ● ● ● ● ●

I was invited to attend our grandsons' out-of-town Little League baseball tournament. The team and their families were housed in a local motel for the weekend, traveling to and from the ball field each day. Unknown to me, our daughter volunteered me to be the "guest preacher" for the team's chapel service on Sunday morning. She informed me of that "assignment" about eight o'clock Saturday night!

At first I was slightly uncomfortable because of the unexpected request and the short notice. But the more I reflected upon the situation, the more positive I began to feel about it. What a marvelous thing to know that a coach of a ten-and-under baseball team would make sure that the boys and their families would have "chapel services" on a Sunday morning away from home.

Not only was the service for the fifteen boys on the team; chapel time was for parents, grandparents, siblings, and friends who might be accompanying them. Everyone gathered above the pool in the hotel lobby for a period of singing, prayer, and a short message—to remember the Lord's Day and to give God thanks. Those who gathered varied in church affiliation. But to the best of my knowledge, *no one skipped out*. Attendance was at 100 percent.

What a heartening event in the midst of rampant secularization! What joy to know that our grandsons have a baseball coach who thinks that Sunday worship is critical for each child. The service might have been simple and short, but the boys were reminded that an important sacred component is a valued ingredient in life.

We are told that we now live in a "post-Christian" age—a time when the power of the secular overshadows much of what once was sacred. A special focus and tenacity is required of us. Hold fast. Don't let the secular crowd out the sacred in your life. If a group of nine- and ten-year-old baseball players can do it, can we do any less?

Prayer: God, give me a sense of the sacred in everything I do this day. Make the journey of this day one full of appreciation for the holy and the good from you.

74. EXTRAVAGANT GRACE

●●●●●●●●●●●●

He spoke before our group twice in two days. Both times, his opening words were the same: "I am a child of the extravagant grace of God." His words held power and obvious conviction. He knew the meaning of that to which he spoke. I know little of his life, but I know this man knows the wonder of God's extravagant grace.

May his words be written across your heart today as well. So much we take for granted! So much of the time we live on the surface of life! So rarely do we appreciate the extravagant grace of God! Day after day, God showers us with this wondrous blessing. Little children put the message in song: "God is so good. God is so good. God is so good, God's so good to me." My granddaughter loves to sing the words now as a mealtime blessing. God is so good—to me and you.

God does not *have* to be so good. God *chooses* to be good. And God chooses to be this way *extravagantly!* Even in difficult days, God extends a loving arm of support. Even in "down" times, God offers an upward turn. Even in life-threatening illness, God's grace promises a life where pain and suffering no longer exist. When you walk through the valleys of disappointment and heartache, the extravagant grace of God is overwhelmingly present.

And in the *good* times? God's abundant grace exceeds all expectations. In the good or relatively easy times, extravagant grace seems most unseen, even unappreciated. "Morning by morning, new mercies I see!" exclaims the hymn writer. Life itself is a gift of grace.

Prayer Focus: Take a quiet moment for a prayer break. Close your eyes and whisper aloud this affirmation and prayer: "I am a child of the extravagant grace of God. Thanks be to God. Amen."

> *From his fullness we have all received, grace upon grace.*
>
> (John 1:16)

75. HOW
DO YOU HANDLE
A HUNGRY SOUL?

•••••••••••••

We enjoy having our grandchildren with us several weeks during the summer. Sometimes in our home; sometimes in other places. Sometimes there are two of them; sometimes there are four. Sometimes they come with their parents; sometimes without. At all times, in all places, and in all numerical constellations, feeding is a constant challenge. The household food budget triples.

The daily feeding frenzy usually begins slowly. Breakfast is not a big issue. But as the day progresses, the momentum accelerates. And every day ends with a large "snack" as the climatic event before bedtime. No exceptions. No variations. Even if dinner happens to be very late, the ritual never varies. Growing children require many feedings. (As I write this, our grandchildren now range from age five through age twelve. I think the *real* challenge may still lie somewhere ahead!)

All growing organisms need to be faithfully fed. What is true for our bodies is even truer for our souls. "Soul food" is the most essential staff of life. You need food for your soul. I need food for my soul. John Wesley's most important contribution to the lives of his followers may have been the insistence upon regular, systematic, life-long soul feeding.

A few moments of personal prayer and a few daily verses of Scripture are soul feeding. Reaching out in love to another person's need feeds your own soul. Combating injustice in the name of a righteous and just God is soul feeding.

You may have the discipline to meet this soul-feeding need on your own. Perhaps you have done so for years, and you will continue to do so. Most of us, however, need the encouragement and support of others. Most of us need a small group of believers who will "watch over us in love" to the end that we do not neglect the feeding of our souls.

Whether alone or with others, do not neglect the feeding of your soul today. Such feeding is the true staff of life.

Prayer Focus: Set a few moments aside on your "calendar" for today to engage in soul feeding. Ask God to help you select the right moment of the day. Perhaps the moment is right now.

76. CLOSER TO GOD

• • • • • • • • • • • •

"Lift me up, Grandpa!" It was our six-year-old grand-daughter who spoke on a leisurely August vacation day. I bent over and picked her up.

"Higher, Grandpa!"

I readily obliged. Our faces met.

"Put me above your head, Grandpa."

With one more upward thrust, I lifted her high into the air and held her there.

"Now, Grandpa," she said, pointing upward with a mischievous glint in her eye, "I'm closer to God than you are!"

The simplicity of her theology momentarily startled me. But I sensed she was right. In the wisdom and wonder of childhood, she was *extraordinarily* close to God—as children commonly are!

Jesus knew this. In a predominantly adult crowd, Jesus affirmed children in order to help us connect with God. "Do you see this child?" he would say on more than one occasion. "This child will teach you what faith is really all about."

Children are extraordinarily important to our faith journey. We teach children so that children can better teach us. We honor children so that children can help us honor God. We celebrate children, who enable us to celebrate God. We elevate children to a high point in our lives so that they can point the way to God for the rest of us.

Closeness to God is a worthy life goal. Children help us toward that goal. Most children are naturally religious. Remember this as you watch your child, grandchild, or friend's child in the next few days. Pray that one or more children will lead *you* to a new stage in your own faith development. Such prayer is both worthy and urgent.

Prayer Focus: Ask God for the privilege of interacting with a preschool child—even briefly—in the next twenty-four hours. Ask God to lead you to a situation where that might be possible. Then let go and learn from those whom Jesus valued most highly.

"Whoever becomes humble like this child is the greatest in the kingdom of heaven. Whoever welcomes one such child in my name welcomes me."
(Matthew 18:4-5)

77. WERE YOU THERE?

●●●●●●●●●●●●

Dr. Martin Marty cites an apparent discrepancy between what American Christians *report* regarding the frequency of their worship versus their *actual* presence in worship. The statistical glitch is both curious and troubling. More Americans report being in worship than actually attend. Why does this phenomenon exist?

One suggestion is that we report on our worship participation as a way of stating our intentions. American church members say to the pollsters, "I really ought to go to worship, and I really intend to go. So put me down as 'having gone,' because next week it will probably be true!"

Another possibility? We *think* we were in worship last Sunday because we used to always attend on a weekly basis. As an "aging" population, we are experiencing short-term memory loss. Since we went to church as children, we habitually think of ourselves as regular worshipers. We may not remember whether we were in worship last Sunday, but we probably were. "So put us down as a yes!" That kind of fudging inflates the statistics!

The truth is this: Current lifestyles and schedules bring

countless interruptions that spoil our worship habits. With millions of other Christians, we are on the road, in the air, on the sea, on the slopes, on the links, or "out to lunch/brunch" during weekend worship hours. If the fault is not our own schedules, then it is that of our children and grandchildren: Soccer tournaments, Little League baseball playoffs, and other events claim our attention.

Worship is the Christian's vital breath. Worship is the energy center for living out the Christian life. Worship is the power base that enables you to cope with the struggles, sorrows, stresses, and crises that intrude upon your life.

Recognize and correct the flow of your discipleship journey. Find the will and the way to "worship weekly unless [truly] prevented"—as John Wesley was quick to advise. Will you be there this weekend—somewhere . . . with a gathered community of believers? And the next? And the next? Establish and celebrate a holy habit in your life!

Prayer Focus: Lift your church (or some local church) up in prayer today. Ask God to use that house of worship in a special way. Visualize yourself in that church for a few moments.

[Do not neglect] to meet together, as is the habit of some, but [encourage] one another.

(Hebrews 10:25)

---

78. CALLING FOR GOD

•••••••••••••

My four-year-old grandson and I were sharing the story of Noah's Ark at bedtime. I read from a large picture book with pull-out flaps which revealed certain characters and animals. He wanted me to read the story several times. Slowly, he savored it. He noticed one repeated phrase: "And God said to Noah. . . ."

"Where is God?" he asked with natural curiosity. "Is this God?" he asked, pointing to a picture of Noah.

"No, that's Noah," I responded. "We can't see God." Then I hastily added, "But anyone can talk to God. And God will talk with you, too."

"Anyone can talk to God?" he queried. "Can I talk to God?"

I responded affirmatively.

"God?" he called out several times from his place on the bed. And then he said, "I don't hear anything. I don't hear God, Poppa."

Next proceeded a lengthy theological discussion between a four-year-old and his grandfather about a God who is not visible to our eyes but who lives in our hearts and who speaks to us in our hearts. I'm not sure how much he grasped. (I never was very good with preschool theology!) But it was a special few moments between us.

There is more to the theological story, of course. Much more. God spoke very definitively two thousand years ago. "Long ago God spoke to our ancestors in many and various ways by the prophets, but in these last days he has spoken to us by a Son," says the writer of Hebrews. Such is the grand and glorious announcement of his coming.

Jesus is the heart of God to the heart of humankind. When we listen to the stories of Jesus, we listen to a God trying to break through to human experience. We sense the heart and the voice of God. This is why Christianity has always advocated "receiving Jesus into your heart."

Receive him today—as you read this. Let your heart prepare him room. Then, when you call out, "God!" you will surely know your call is heard. And your heart will know that God has already answered.

Prayer Focus: Close your eyes for a moment. Say (or sing) these words: "Come into my heart, Lord Jesus. There is room in my heart for you." Welcome him as your gracious Companion for the day.

"Be strong and courageous; do not be frightened or dismayed, for the LORD *your God is with you wherever you go."*

(Joshua 1:9)

---

79. HOW'S YOUR "HAND WRITING"?

• • • • • • • • • • • •

A national news magazine reports a serious deterioration in our handwriting today. In fact, ten million letters a year end up in the "dead letter office" because neither machine nor human eyes can decipher the handwriting on the envelope. That is a lot of "dead letters"! Just imagine all the short notes, the "keeping in touch" letters and the presumed bill payments that are permanently "lost." Just imagine how many love letters never find that "significant other"!

I know something about this phenomenon. I won a handwriting award in grade school many years ago. However, my handwriting has moved rapidly downhill since those days. While in college, I did all of my correspondence on a typewriter—including letters home. My "love letter" correspondence with my fiancée (now my wife) was done on a typewriter. (Although I *did* sign my name!) Today, all letters, all notes, all material that I *really want to be read* I do by word-processor or e-mail. Reading my handwriting is a chore at best and impossible at worst!

You and I are called by God to deliver a letter of love

to every human being with whom we may be in contact. We must not risk having the "love letter" end up in a dead-letter box somewhere because it is illegible or un-communicative. We must ensure that it is clear, relevant, and attention-grabbing. We must be ever vigilant with our "hand writing."

Know this as a certainty: *The message is worth delivering!*

Prayer Focus: Ask God to guide you to write one *handwritten* note of appreciation to someone today. Make it brief and legible. Include some reference to prayer or spiritual encouragement in the note. Send it on its way with prayer.

And you show that you are a letter of Christ, prepared by us, written not with ink but with the Spirit of the living God, not on tablets of stone but on tablets of human hearts.

(2 Corinthians 3:3)

---

80. NEVER POWER-LESS!

●●●●●●●●●●●●●

Several dozen church newsletters arrive at my desk weekly. A few are unsolicited, but most come from colleagues I have known over the years. One January, newsletters from the south-central section of the nation carried the same theme: terrible ice storms. The details were very similar: massive power failures in wide areas; lights, telephones, cooking facilities, garage door openers, and church organs that didn't work. Some reported the details the news media had already delivered: crops destroyed or severely damaged.

The situation with an ice storm is quickly out of control! Nothing can be done—except wait.

Apparently, many storms occur on Saturday night or Sunday morning. Such timing, of course, prompts the topic of conversation and ready-made themes for pastor's columns. A few colleagues treat the matter lightheartedly. Some tell personal stories of how they or their homes were affected. One lamented, "No coffee pot, no computer, no radio or TV, no morning shower, no hot meal!"

The good news of the Christian journey is that the Power never fails. One promise you can trust is one spoken at least three times early in the Old Testament: "It is the LORD who goes before you. He will be with you; he will not fail you or forsake you. Do not fear or be dismayed" (Deuteronomy 31:8). The key promise is clear: God will not fail you or forsake you!

To live in the wake of that promise is to live with courage and optimism. In a relationship with God, things are never out of control. The power is never compromised. God invites you to that kind of connection on your daily walk.

I cannot imagine what life would be like without the encouraging, enduring, encompassing power of God in the midst of my life. In his Spirit, things are never out of control. You are never without God, the greatest Power Source of all.

Prayer: God, grant me the power that endlessly flows from you. Help me to know that I can be connected to you every moment—and with incredible positive results.

81. SHEER WONDER

•••••••••••••

Uncounted millenniums ago, a huge glacier cut its way through the mountainous terrain of the Sierra Nevadas in what is now eastern California. The impact of that glacial movement yielded a legacy of beauty and richness that is staggering in its visual impact. Today we call it Yosemite National Park.

The Yosemite Valley is a work of sheer wonder. Towering walls of solid granite stand everywhere, with honored names such as El Capitan, Half Dome, Three Brothers, and Cathedral Rock. Thunderous waterfalls cascade into the valley during the early summer months from the mountain's winter snow melt. The Merced River winds its way through the valley floor. To be in Yosemite Valley is to be linked to the power of a glacial age, the gentle ordering of ecology and environment, and the lasting beauty of God's creation.

Two millenniums ago, one named Jesus cut a path through human history that is unique and unparalleled. The impact of his coming yields a legacy of power and richness that is similarly staggering in its visual, intellectual, and experiential stimulation.

To be linked to Jesus of Nazareth is to be linked to the richness of sacred history, the full experience of meaning and purpose, and a way of life that is the highest and best we will ever know.

Thank God for the visual wonder of Yosemite Valley. Thank God even more for the wondrous gift of Jesus to the world.

Prayer Focus: Give thanks to God for Jesus. Invite Jesus into the center of your activities today. Receive him as if drawing a deep breath. Walk with the confidence that his companionship brings you.

82. STAYING CLOSE TO GOOD FRIENDS

•••••••••••••

Wherever one of our grandsons travels, no matter how short the distance, he carries a knapsack full of "guys" with him. The guys are little plastic figures. They are the heroes of television, movies, and storybooks. Some are cartoon characters from many creators.

He possesses scores of these little figures. They travel with him to Grandpa's house. They also travel with him to a restaurant table, to the bathtub, and to bed at night. Soon after his arrival in a new location, the guys are emptied from his knapsack. Several favorites emerge for some animated play. When it is time to relocate, the guys are returned to the knapsack and are carried to the new station.

He knows each one by name. He knows their story. He knows they are his friends.

Dozens of Bible characters are your friends. They teach you God-centered living. They give you courage. They help you retain honesty and optimism about living. How helpful to know their names, to know their stories, to know them as friends!

How helpful to know the adventurous spirit of Abraham, the leadership vision of Moses, the transformed humanity of Peter, and the passionate conviction of Paul. How wonderful to know the creative instincts of Miriam, the trust of Mary, the patience of Anna, or the kindnesses of Dorcas.

These, and so many others, are the "guys" (and gals) who have been pioneers in the faith. They are woven into the fabric of our faith tradition. They are part of God's story for us. They are your guides for the journey. They are friends for the abundant life found in Jesus.

One night, our little grandson dumped a bulging knapsack of "guys" into the whirlpool bathtub one more time. And I thought: How precious are the saints of God. How impoverished we are when we do not know them— or their stories!

Prayer Focus: Give thanks to God for pioneers in faith who have gone before you. Close with thanks for Jesus— whom Scripture calls the "pioneer and perfecter" of our faith (Hebrews 12:2).

All the saints greet you.

(2 Corinthians 13:12*b*)

83. ORGANICALLY GROWN

• • • • • • • • • • • •

For many years I have been an organic gardener on a small scale: natural mulch from the yard as opposed to chemical fertilizers; a few strange combinations of flowers among the vegetables to ward off pests (marigolds among the beans, nasturtiums among the squash).

The small piece of ground is very special to me. I can spend a day there, or an hour, or twenty minutes. But that bit of land stimulates the juices of awe and wonder on a regular basis. I learn from the land. I care about it. I put myself into it. I draw from it. It is my little corner of God's earth.

Of special fascination to me is how the Bible speaks about the land. Care for the "garden" is not just a random issue. You and I are a part of the land. Somewhere along the way, we began to believe that we are separate from the land. Nothing could be a greater error. We are a part of the land, the soil, the earth.

But we are more, much more. We also are spiritual beings in these "clay pots." Paul writes, "But we have this treasure in clay jars, so that it may be made clear that this extraordinary power belongs to God and does not come from us" (2 Corinthians 4:7). What a great verse for those who like to get their hands in the soil!

Know both your earthiness and your uniqueness as a creation of God. And rejoice!

Prayer Focus: Examine your hands for a moment as "flesh and bones." Then clasp your hands together and give thanks for the miracle of God being within you.

84. TOO MANY CHOICES

•••••••••••••

One year I received an even dozen seed catalogues in one week in January. I had never known such a glut of catalogues. Was competition growing dramatically? Were new entrepreneurs on the loose in the seed production business? Did the same marketing strategist suggest that client companies buy lists with my name on them? Did the purveyors of seeds in this nation expect me to divide my somewhat meager $40 order among nine companies?

I browsed them all—and then ordered from "old faithful"—the same company I had used for years, and my father before me!

Don't misunderstand! I enjoy adventure. I covet an occasional challenge or a creative new possibility. God is full of limitless surprise. However, that year "the glut of catalogues" reminded me of the call toward retrenchment, toward discipleship basics. In that call may be the steady call of God for each of us.

I want to stay on course, for the course seems substantial and worthy. I want to use the best of what I already know. I want to make sure that the "tried-and-true" seeds are planted well, in good soil, and given a chance to flourish.

You do not need to be innovative and fresh in every new day of discipleship. You may find great comfort in a few familiar pattern prayers, in a simple devotional reading, or in the same time and place for weekly worship. Perhaps you even find comfort in the same church pew!

You will want to freshen your spiritual growth diet from time to time. You also will want to remember those growth options that have served you well. Cultivate those basic disciplines toward maximum fruition. Gradually, and with genuine anticipation, you then may move on to new ventures among God's abundant possibilities.

Prayer Focus: Make a short list of "what works for you"—what helps you to grow spiritually. Give thanks to God for that list. Exercise one item on that list during the next few minutes.

> *Surely God is my salvation; / I will trust, and will not be afraid, / for the LORD GOD is my strength and my might; / he has become my salvation.*
> (Isaiah 12:2)

85. KNOCK, KNOCK!

●●●●●●●●●●●●

Someone gave my six-year-old grandson a book of "knock, knock" jokes for Christmas. He was full of them while we visited during the holiday week. His telling of them was almost as humorous as some of the jokes themselves.

"Knock, knock, Grandpa."

"Who's there?"

"Freddie!"

"Freddie who?"

"Freddie or not, here I come!" (Followed by a deep and resonant, "Ho, Ho!" as though to say, "Gotcha!")

His four-year-old brother occasionally got into the act, mostly as an echo of his older sibling.

The sacred voice of Scripture has its own "knock, knock" story. "Listen! I am standing at the door, knocking" (Revelation 3:20). The deeply personal God who is Lord of life and history yearns for the invitation to enter your life more deeply. Even when you have spoken the yes of faith, God still knocks at an interior door. God seeks the inmost and broadest expanse of your life.

Enter into the adventure of a growing faith. Offer a prayer of thanks to the One who knocks at the door of your heart and calls you to walk with greater faithfulness.

Prayer: God, let me sense you knocking at the door of the deepest within me right now. Let my life be one of ever opening toward you.

86. MAKING CONNECTIONS

●●●●●●●●●●●●●

As a young boy, I was always reminded to leave a snack for Santa under the tree each Christmas Eve before bedtime. It was always the same snack: a ripe banana, a couple of chocolate chip cookies, and a tall glass of cold milk. I would head off for bed in the secure knowledge that Santa would be well fed at my house that night.

As the years passed, however, I began to make the connection. My father's favorite bedtime snack? A ripe banana, a couple of chocolate chip cookies, and a tall glass of cold milk. I wonder now at the slow growth in that awareness in my childhood. It took a long time for the correlation to be apparent.

The Christian gospel is the grand announcement that God has made a clear and gracious connection with our humanity. Yet we are often very slow to correlate this Good News with the realities of his coming. We hold on to some fantasy or make-believe interpretation of life. We are inundated with competing claims for our attention. We seldom stop to consider the greater truth.

In Jesus, the connection is made visible. The Christ event is a concrete moment in recorded history. Jesus entered your history. Jesus lived as a man in the midst of humankind. He struggled, prayed, and worshiped God. He modeled a faithful image of what God intends. He conquered the last great enemy of life—death itself. He is Emmanuel, the God who is with us. There can be no doubt about it! The bridge and the eternal bond between Creator and creation is real.

Rejoice in the discovery and rediscovery of that extraordinary connection. Celebrate the connection with exceptional joy. Never let yourself be dissuaded otherwise.

Prayer: Thank you, God, for the mystery of your connection to me, and of me to you. That connection is a wonder I do not fully understand, but one that I celebrate nonetheless!

God chose to make known . . . the riches of the glory of this mystery, which is Christ in you, the hope of glory.

(Colossians 1:27)

---

87. WHAT WILL THEY SAY?

● ● ● ● ● ● ● ● ● ● ● ●

A distant relative put together a genealogy of my paternal ancestors. He traced the family back to a small town in Germany in the 1500s. In the opening portion of the book, he included a translation of a sermon delivered upon the death of a member of the family who died in A.D. 1550. The eulogy is a marvelous four-page testimony to the power and witness of her faithful Christian life.

The deceased made no specific mark on history. Her name is not recorded in any history book. But her witness was clear: She lived a memorable demonstration of a Christ-like life.

Your most durable legacy to the future is not your estate, your embroidery, your business acumen, or your social graces. Your legacy is that of having demonstrated something of the presence of Jesus in your life. That is all God asks of you or any of us. And in that living, God's heart is made glad.

Prayer: Let the beauty of Jesus be seen in me this day, O Lord.

88. SHELTER

●●●●●●●●●●●●

One of the great hymns of faith was written by Martin Luther: "A mighty fortress is our God, a bulwark never failing." Many people do not know what a *bulwark* is. A bulwark is any protection against external danger.

My father arrived in Pittsburgh, Pennsylvania, in the mid 1930s with the Army Corps of Engineers. He was assigned to oversee the construction of locks and dams on the rivers. These locks and dams are flood control systems. Obviously, they do not protect the city from all flooding, but they do protect it from terrible disaster. They are a bulwark against flooding rivers.

Sometimes storms enter your life very quickly. Some searing tragedy cuts across your life without any advance warning. Some high wind strikes with such force as to uproot you entirely.

What is *your* bulwark?

Knowing the God revealed in Jesus is critical to spiritual survival in the midst of such storms. Abraham Lincoln once said, "I have been driven many times to my knees by the overwhelming conviction that I had nowhere else to go."

Your first priority is to be connected to God. *That* is your bulwark. That connection is better than a good light and safer than a known way.

Prayer: "Rock of Ages, cleft for me, let me hide myself in thee" (Augustus M. Toplady, 1776).

> *I said to the man who stood at the gate of the year, "Give me a light that I may tread safely into the unknown." And he replied: "Go out into the darkness and put your hand into the hand of God. That shall be to you better than light and safer than a known way."*
>
> (King George VI of England,
> in a radio broadcast on December 25, 1939,
> quoting Minnie Louise Haskins' "God Knows")

89. CITY SLICKERS

• • • • • • • • • • • •

In the movie *City Slickers,* two middle-aged men decide to work out their midlife crisis by spending two weeks on a ranch in the West. One of the men is played by Billy Crystal. An old cowboy whom they meet is played by Jack Palance. Here is my recollection of a conversation that takes place between Crystal and Palance:

Palance: Yeah, you all come out here about the same age. Same problems. Spend fifty weeks a year getting knots in your rope, then you think two weeks up here will untie them for you. None of you get it. (*long pause*) Do you know what the secret of life is?
Crystal: No, what?
Palance: This! (*He holds up his index finger.*)
Crystal: Your finger?
Palance: One thing, just one thing. You stick to that, and everything else doesn't mean a thing.
Crystal: That's great, but what's the one thing?
Palance: That's what you've got to figure out.

Life is about living in God. Live your life as a piece of this truth. Rest in God. In this one thing, you will find nobility of spirit and zest for living.

Prayer Focus: For just a few moments, imagine yourself held comfortably in the cup of God's hand. Then imagine yourself being "let go" to live today in the reality of Who is really in charge!

90. SPIRITUAL OVERFLOW

●●●●●●●●●●●●

If there is a spiritual emptiness in America, it is because we are trusting the gods of prosperity, growth, and possessions. A Chinese proverb reads, "No image maker worships the gods he makes because he knows the stuff of which they are made."

Most of us don't need one more gadget or one more piece of furniture. Yet, as John Updike reminds us, "In America, it is difficult to achieve a sense of enough."

Jesus encourages us to get out from under any trust in possessions, resources, or wealth. These things may be *used* by God. But they will not make you happy. More of Jesus' parables are devoted to money and possessions than any other theme. Things will never set you on an eternal course of happiness. When you trust in the possessions you own, you always will come up empty.

Medical researchers are now finding scientific proof for what Jesus taught long ago. Giving to others is a form of receiving. Giving persons actually heighten their overall zest for living and increase their life expectancy. Love remains the only gift that multiplies when you give it away.

Life outside of self is the only durable way to live.

Prayer Focus: Ask God to show you some way to give away something of yourself today. Ask to be shown *what* you are to give and *to whom* it is to be given.

91. BOLDLY EXPECTANT PRAYER

•••••••••••••

In your prayer life, there is certainly a time for quiet prayer. There is a time for centering upon God in silence. But some occasions call for crying out, for speaking aloud to God. Moments of pain! Moments of frustration! Moments of desperate concern for another! Moments of the seeming absence of God!

Find a space where you can speak aloud with God without being heard by another person. That space might be in your automobile, an empty house, or the out-of-doors. There are times to cry aloud, to shout. Such prayer is acceptable to God.

In fact, God invites you to be bold, specific, persistent, and (on occasion) loud with your prayers. Be as specific as you care to be. Pray as often as you will, over and over again.

Always, you are encouraged to pray with expectation. You are given the privilege of praying expectantly. God hears and responds. God does not always respond in exactly the way you ask. But God always responds with good.

When you pray, come to Jesus with bold expectation.

Such prayer not only will reach the ears of God but also will transform you. And know this: It is the inner transformation that gives the Christian life its essential quality.

Prayer Focus: Find some place to talk to God out loud today! Name some passion or concern and speak about it before God as you would converse with a trusted friend.

92. A WARM REBOOT

•••••••••••

We can learn a spiritual truth from some specific computer language. When you reboot a computer, you essentially restart the whole system. Computers sometimes get hopelessly tied up in their own internal processes. Their "thinking" gets befuddled or worse. So you reboot the computer. Computer students distinguish between a "cold" reboot and a "warm" reboot.

In a cold reboot, you turn the computer completely off and restart it again. Such a procedure is not really desirable, but sometimes necessary. It is the only thing that seems to work.

However, you also can exercise a "warm" reboot. In this procedure, you can restart the computer without going through the radical step of shutting down completely. A warm reboot also can free the computer from tangled circuits.

Jesus came to give us a warm reboot in life. He came to give your life a fresh, exciting new flow.

Consider another useful image.

Have you ever traveled down a four-lane divided highway and suddenly discovered that you were going in the wrong direction? All the signs say "No U-turn." So you keep driving and looking. Finally, you may come to a break in the divider and a sign that says "U-turns Permitted."

Jesus extends the invitation to you: U-turns permitted here! You are both invited and permitted. Jesus gives you a warm reboot. We can move in a new direction. That's the promise and the hope.

Most of us have no idea of our potential. Jesus calls us to do what we never imagined we could.

Jesus invites you to walk in a new direction. He gives you the invitation, the permission, and the power to make that choice.

Prayer: Gracious God, where do I need a warm reboot in my life right now? Help me to see where that place is and then take your hand in a full U-turn. Help me to walk in a new direction in that part of my life.

93. STANDING UP "ON THE INSIDE"

•••••••••••••

A little boy was shopping with his father in a department store. They came to a mannequin made of inflated plastic. The little boy took a swing at the mannequin. The figure fell to the floor and then bounced upright again. The child was startled. He reached back and hit the inflated figure again. Again the mannequin fell backwards to the floor and then immediately stood upright.

"Daddy," the child asked, "why does the man stand up again after I hit him?"

"I don't know," the father replied. "Why do you think it happens?"

The boy thought for a moment and then said, "Maybe it's because he is standing up on the inside."

Jesus does not care about the outer arrangements of your life. But Jesus does care about the inside. Jesus invites you to stand up on the inside and thereby enter the life of the Kingdom.

Prayer Focus: Give your "inside"—your heart, your thoughts, your feelings—to God today for any necessary reworking and transformation.

"The greatest among you must become like the youngest, and the leader like one who serves."
(Luke 22:26)

94. EASTER MAKES A DIFFERENCE RIGHT NOW!

● ● ● ● ● ● ● ● ● ● ● ●

Somewhere in the country, a social service agency sent out a letter to a recipient of their services: "We have received notice that you are deceased. Your food stamps will be stopped effective immediately. You may reapply if there is any change in your circumstances."

Consider the story of Easter for a moment. The Easter message means that there *has* been a change in our circumstances. A change has occurred in the way you live your life right now. Easter is not the "grand finale" of faith. Easter is more of an overture to the greatest symphony of all time. Easter is not the end point; it is the beginning point.

Prayer: Thank you, God, for giving me *life* right now, today, in this moment.

> *Surely the* LORD *is in this place—and I did not know it!*
>
> (Genesis 28:16)

95. BAPTIZED

•••••••••••••

Personal identity is somehow blurred today. We are unsure about gender identity, about masculine and feminine roles, about roles as husbands and wives. Some are unsure of racial, ethnic, or national origin. Many persons crave a knowledge of their genetic origins. Adults who were adopted as children move in a passionate search for their birth parents.

For the Christian, one identity surpasses all others. One identity is far more important than genes or gender or ethnicity. This identity is more important than being chief executive officer, lead teacher, chairperson of the board, or superintendent of the Sunday school. Here is an identity that is more important than grandparent or parent or husband or wife.

One identity exceeds all others: You are claimed as a child of God! When you profess your belief in Jesus Christ and are baptized, you begin to walk with the most important identity that a life can know.

You have a birth certificate. That document remains important. You will need to retrieve it from time to time for some particular purpose.

Once you have been baptized, you also have a baptismal certificate. Value your baptismal certificate more than your birth certificate. Your baptismal certificate is your *primary* identification!

Tomorrow morning, when you awaken, walk to the sink in the bathroom, splash cold water on your face three times, and say, "I am [or *I want to be*] baptized—in the name of the Father, the Son, and the Holy Spirit. Thanks be to God." Make that experience a morning ritual in your life.

Prayer Focus: If you have been baptized, try to locate your baptismal certificate. Hold it in your hand and give thanks to God for this primary identification in your life. If you have not been baptized, talk with God about taking this important step in your faith journey.

96. VALLEYS

• • • • • • • • • • • •

Most of us walk through a series of valleys in a lifetime. Sometimes the valley is the loss of a job or a marriage or a friendship. Sometimes it is the loss of a family member through death. Sometimes it is one of life's most painful losses—the loss of a child, whether that child be very young or an adult. Sometimes the loss is related to mobility or health. Occasionally, the loss is the future—when the future is literally "yanked" out from under you. Eventually, the loss is experienced in facing your own death.

Life is full of shoulder-stooping, sleep-robbing, heart-breaking valleys.

The good news is that *you do not walk the valleys alone*. You do not walk by yourself through the valley. This is the divine promise. The message for the believer's walk is that you have a Companion in the valley. Faith in Jesus as the Companion in the valley is the protest of hope against all evidence for despair.

Notice the good word in a familiar psalm: "Even though I walk *through* the darkest valley" (23:4*a*, emphasis added). God does not simply let us walk *in* the valley. God always walks with us *through* the valley.

Prayer Focus: Say these words aloud as an affirmation of faith: "Even though I walk through the valley, I know that you are the Companion of the way with me."

> *The LORD is my shepherd. . . .*
>
> (Psalm 23:1)

97. RISK

●●●●●●●●●●●●

Jesus invites you to risk. If you are like me, you are not particularly prone to take a lot of risks. William James describes most Americans as "pragmatists"—we must know the consequences of something before we act.

Most of us don't like risk. We don't like a lot of change.

Disciples of Jesus don't have to be pragmatists. We don't have to know the consequences of every decision we make or action we take. The walk of faith is the walk of risk. But it is well-grounded risk because it is at the invitation of Jesus.

Most Christians have very little notion of what God can do through us. We probably have only a small notion of our capabilities. Jesus called men and women to do things they never thought they would do.

Living as a Christian is one risky adventure after another. Jesus stands in front of you, calling you forward. Jesus stands behind you, gently nudging. And Jesus stands beside you, as Friend.

Prayer Focus: Ask God to give you greater freedom and comfort in taking risks. Ask God to clarify the kinds of risk appropriate to your level of faith. Jot down any answers or hints of an answer you may receive.

98. "GROW LIGHT"

For many years, I started vegetables and seeds indoors in late winter under something called a "grow light." The light looked much like a florescent bulb, but it was considerably more expensive. The light emitted from the bulb gave plants a strong start.

In a recent summer, my wife and I visited friends in Maine. As we approached their home, I noticed that his vegetable garden was considerably ahead of mine. When I commented about the matter (with a twinge of jealousy), he said, "Yes, and you know that we only have about 60 days of summer here—from June 15 to August 15."

"Then how in the world does your garden do so well?" I inquired. "How can your garden be ahead of mine with even less summer growing season?"

With a smile, he replied, "You forget that we have two extra hours of daylight here every day. The added light makes the plants grow and mature faster."

Jesus is the ultimate miracle of light. Jesus is the light for any and all darkness. He is the light for the next few steps and for the long haul. He is the one light that does not burn out and that never turns off. He is the welcoming light at the end of the tunnel. His light brings growth and maturity to your life.

Prayer Focus: Close your eyes and image yourself bathed in the light from above. Feel the warmth, the nurturing power of that light. Before you open your eyes, breathe a prayer of thanks to God for the ultimately significant light.

In him was life, and the life was the light of all people. The light shines in the darkness, and the darkness did not overcome it.

(John 1:4-5)

99. TOUGH TIMBER

• • • • • • • • • • • •

A group of mountain hikers came across an old woodsman carrying an ax on his shoulder. "Where are you going?" they asked.

"I'm headed up the mountain to get some wood for repairs to my cabin," he replied.

"But why are you going up the mountain? There is wood to be found everywhere you look right here!"

"Oh, no," came the quick reply. "I need the timber from the higher elevations—where the wood is hard and toughened by the weather. I need to go up higher where the strong timber grows."

Your faith is the tough timber of your life. Faith can be shaken a bit at times. You can be momentarily out of touch with God. But faith can never be taken away.

Faith makes it possible to live without fear. Faith is a willingness to laugh at fear. Faith is the strong timber for tumultuous times.

Your faith walk is tough, fearless, and loaded with mystery. But it is the walk of a healthy soul.

Prayer Focus: Give thanks to God for someone who has modeled faith for you—either recently or long ago.

| *"Do not be afraid."* | (Luke 2:10) |

---

100. DO NOT FORGET!

● ● ● ● ● ● ● ● ● ● ● ●

One of the ways in which you honor God is with your memory. "Bless the LORD, O my soul, / and do not forget all his benefits," cries the psalmist (103:2). You honor and bless God by remembering what God has done. You praise God by calling to mind the many benefits God bestows.

Honor God by remembering grace freely given. Honor God by remembering that you are forgiven. Honor God with your gratitude.

A woman wrote of her bout with cancer and the role of her faith: "I committed myself to follow Jesus nineteen years ago. Now, the unexpected bursts of gratitude that invade me are moments of resurrection."

Live the next few days with bursts of gratitude. Honor God by remembering all that God has done. Remember what God *is* doing and *wants* to do in your life.

Prayer Focus: Pray this psalm three times: "Bless the LORD, O my soul, / and all that is within me, / bless [God's] holy name" (103:1).

101. WITH GOD . . .

•••••••••••••

I cannot recall where I read these words: "We are not blessed with an escape from the harsh realities of life, but we are favored with the Presence of a God who can transform us in the midst of these realities."

A similar quotation from my seminary classroom has nourished me for more than three decades: "God does not will everything that happens, but in every thing that happens, God wills good!"(John Godsey, Fall 1961, Drew Theological School).

Both of these statements urge a relationship with God—a daily, disciplined relationship! When you hold God's hand, when you develop a relationship with God, when you cultivate a friendship with God, all things are possible.

Prayer: "I can do all things *through [the One] who strengthens me*" (Philippians 4:13, emphasis added).

[God] by the power at work within us is able to accomplish abundantly far more than all we can ask or imagine.

(Ephesians 3:20)
